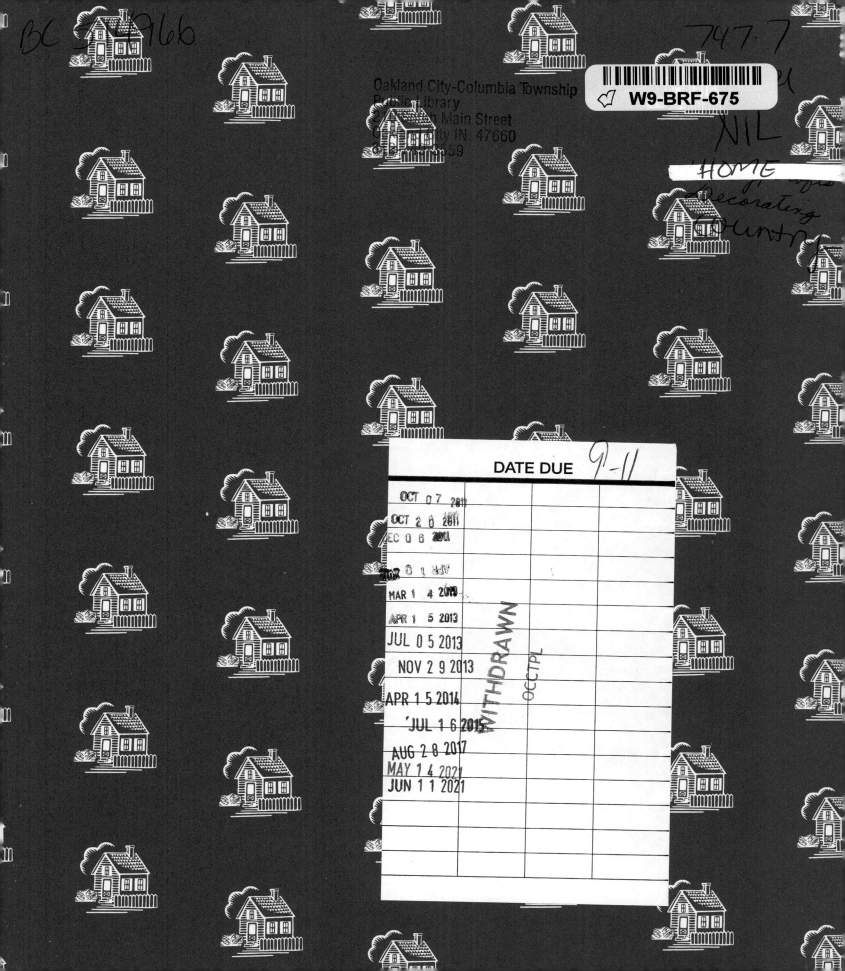

Country Living
COUNTRY
Decorating

Country Living

COUNTRY
Decorating

Bo Niles

Hearst Books

New York

Library of Congress Cataloging-in-Publication Data

Country Living country decorating/by Bo Niles

p. cm.
Includes index
ISBN 0-688-08073-1
1. Interior decoration. 2. Decoration and ornament, Rustic.
3. Antiques in interior decoration. I. Niles, Bo. II.
Country living (New York, N.Y.) III. Title: Country
decorating.
NK 1986.R8C67 1988
747.213 —dc19   88-4112
                                                       CIP

Printed in Singapore

First Edition

1 2 3 4 5 6 7 8 9 10

COUNTRY LIVING STAFF
Rachel Newman, *Editor*
Bo Niles, *Senior Editor*
Niña Williams, *Editor At Large*

PRODUCED BY SMALLWOOD AND STEWART,
NEW YORK CITY

Designed by Sue Rose

Typeset by Village Type & Graphics,
New York City

Contents

INTRODUCTION 8

THE HEART OF COUNTRY LIVING 10

LIVING THE COUNTRY LIFE 26

COUNTRY LIVING ROOMS

LOG LIVING ROOMS

ONE-ROOM LIVING   ANTIQUE RUGS

THE COLORFUL LIVING ROOM   ADVERTISING ART

CASUAL LIVING ROOMS   THE WING CHAIR

THE SHAKER LEGACY   COUNTRY IN THE CITY

DISPLAYING COLLECTIONS   DECOYS

TABLE DISPLAYS   SUMMER LIVING ROOMS

ANTIQUE LINENS   FOLK ART

COUNTRY DINING ROOMS

THE KEEPING ROOM   HOMESPUNS

FORMAL DINING ROOMS   ANTIQUE BASKETS

WOODENWARE   INFORMAL DINING ROOMS

POTTERY & CERAMICS   THE COLORFUL DINING ROOM

PORCH DINING   COUNTRY TABLES

COUNTRY KITCHENS

RUSTIC KITCHENS

KITCHEN COLLECTIONS

THE WOOD STOVE, THE PIE SAFE

THE COLORFUL KITCHEN

ENTRANCES

HALLS & FOYERS   GAMEBOARDS   STAIRWAYS

THE COUNTRY BEDROOM

ROMANTIC BEDROOMS   THE FOUR-POSTER BED

BED HANGINGS   THE COLORFUL BEDROOM

DECORATING WITH QUILTS   BED- LIVING ROOMS

TURKEYWORK   GUEST ROOMS   COVERLETS

CHILDREN'S ROOMS   DOLLS & TOYS

TEDDY BEARS

THE OUTDOORS

OPEN PORCHES   ENCLOSED PORCHES

A SUMMER SCREENED HOUSE   GARDEN ROOMS

GARDEN FURNISHINGS   GARDENS

A SUMMER PLAYHOUSE

CREATING THE COUNTRY LOOK 186

COUNTRY CRAFTS

THE SCHOOLHOUSE: A SYMBOL OF COUNTRY

A SCHOOLHOUSE QUILT   THE BASKET QUILT

CARING FOR QUILTS   LINENS & LACE

CROSS-STITCH   CANDLEWICK BEDSPREAD

COUNTRY PAINT TECHNIQUES

THE ART OF STENCILING

PENNY RUGS   HOOKED RUGS

DRIED FLOWERS & POTPOURRIS

WREATHS   ICE CANDLES

A COUNTRY SOURCEBOOK   244

INDEX   252

PICTURE CREDITS   254

ACKNOWLEDGMENTS   256

Introduction

In the autumn of 1978, a new magazine was born: *Country Living*. Two years before, the American Bicentennial had refocussed our attention on all things American. But in the following year, *American Home*, a 60-year-old magazine dedicated to American living, had expired, after several volatile years of mistaken identity. John Mack Carter, who had once led *American Home* and was now editor of *Good Housekeeping*, felt there was a place for a new magazine that would speak, once again, of an all-American way of life and a truly American lifestyle. Thus, he came up with the concept of *Country Living* magazine.

The success of the first, test issue of *Country Living* confirmed that there was indeed a broad-based, enthusiastic audience for this kind of magazine. At this time, John Mack Carter invited me to join him at *Good Housekeeping*, to develop *Country Living*. Our goal: to create a monthly magazine that would address all aspects of country, from traditional to contemporary, from every part of America.

As an indication that we've achieved our goal, *Country Living* magazine has become one of the largest "shelter"—or home-oriented—magazines in the United States, with a circulation of over 1.8 million readers. *Country Living* has been one of the fastest-growing publications in magazine history.

Why *Country Living*?

Country Living grew out of a real need. *Country Living* reconfirms and reaffirms a uniquely American way of living—and, in words and photographs, expresses a uniquely American style of decorating. In an era of high-technology, nuclear proliferation, and the breakdown of many revered institutions, *Country Living* has evolved as a magazine that speaks of home, heart, and hearth, to enduring and real family values and to what we call a high-touch way of life.

In many ways, too, we remind people of a gentler time, when life was less chaotic. *Country Living* embraces nostalgia and sentiment—but is not sentimental. In a "cold" environment, *Country Living* is committed to bringing warmth back into our readers' lives. We consider our readers family, and they, in turn, think of us as family. They invite us into their homes, and, when we feature their homes, we—and they—invite everyone who looks at our pages to enter and feel comfortable and at home there with us.

Country Living speaks of involvement: involvement with home, with family, with friends, and with the community, and with the world.

We long to preserve our land and its bounty. Enduring love of land and country has molded this nation. *Country Living* honors traditions and values as an antidote to the trendy which insinuates obsolescence. *Country Living*, by contrast, offers continuity and security.

Restoration, renovation, and collecting are at the heart of the country homestyle, and signify connections to family, to roots, and to personal heritage. A home that expresses connection is relaxed and comfortable. A home that expresses connection is joyful and full of love.

To celebrate joy and love, and our connection to you, we have chosen our favorite rooms and places for this, our 10th Anniversary book, which we have called *COUNTRY LIVING COUNTRY DECORATING*. Here the country lifestyle and country homestyle come together, to give you the best we have to offer: a connection—from us to you.

Rachel Newman

The Heart of

COUNTRY

Living

Country. It's a simple word, it seems, but just what does it mean? What is Country?

Country resonates with associations, some literal, some symbolic, some rooted in emotion.

First, of course, country means nation, where we come from, where we live, that land we identify ourselves with. Country, in the context of this book, is America.

Country also connotes a sense of place or a sense of the natural environment. Country is mountains and marshland, plains and desert, riverbank and oceanfront. Country is the rural outdoors.

But the concept of country runs deeper than patriotism or ecology. Country, over the course of the last decade or so, has come to signify and symbolize both a lifestyle and a homestyle—and it has come to describe a way of decorating as well.

With the birth of our magazine, *Country Living*, a term was coined to embrace a uniquely American decorating style—and an attitude or state of mind. The term, Country, suddenly and clearly brought into focus a homestyle and lifestyle that had, in fact, endured for not only generations, but, in the purest "roots" sense, for centuries.

Many Americans find in Country a reaffirmation and a reconfirmation of the way they actually lived, or the way their parents lived, or the way they remember— or were told—their grandparents, great-grandparents, and ancestors lived.

In terms of decorating, Country initiated a trend for those unfamiliar with its elements; for countless others, country reinforced notions about making their houses comfortable in a uniquely American way.

A decade ago, *Country Living* had a vision of a homestyle that hearkened back to a gentle, innocent past. Country was perceived as a refreshing antidote to high-technology and streamlined modernism. And Country reasserted a focus on family values.

The appreciation of Country coincided with a yearning for a seminal version of the American Dream: to live in a simple place with simple furnishings, in a simple and unaffected way. Though romanticized, the yearning was—and is—very real: the spirit of Country centers on the home.

Homemade, homespun, homegrown. These words capture the values of the country style. Those pioneer values of fortitude, honesty, strength in the face of adversity, and communion with family and friends underscored and lent energy to the Country style.

The elements of Country are now icons: primitive handmade furnishings dressed in their original paint or smoothed to a well-worn patina by use; homespun fabrics exhibiting plain weaves, gritty textures, and robust earthy colors, or displaying gentle miniature prints in pretty hues; woodburning stoves and hearty homemade foods; and handmade crafts, often indigenous to America, such as quilts, hooked rugs, and folk art.

The popularity of country living has spawned an interest in flea markets and rural auctions, and long-overlooked pieces have been snapped up by eager collectors who sincerely wanted to touch America and American things. But if these things were American, where did they come from—and why?

The roots of Americana and American design do not date only from 1776, just as they do not date only from the Plymouth colony or the fortified community of Jamestown. Because America was vast and open, uncharted and undeveloped, waves of settlers from many lands came here and established their own roots. As one group acquired wealth and status, yet another wave of immigrants—often, as in the seventeenth century, less privileged—arrived, fanning out further and further across the nation. As they pioneered, homesteaded, and tamed a seemingly endless frontier, Americana was reborn over and over and over again. Unlike an elite design motif which emerges as a single style, comes to a crescendo, and subsides over the course of a decade or single generation, the elemental American homestyle endured and flourished.

The taut, tight homestead itself, for instance, was recreated again and again in various guises. In the South and Midwest, it was constructed of logs; in the Southwest it was molded of adobe; on the Great Plains it was hacked out of sod. Furnishings, too, were hand-built; they were rough, rude, primitive—and often multipurpose. American design, in the frontier sense, was constant and practical.

Country, as it was rediscovered and revived a decade ago, looked primarily to an Anglo-American design heritage. The pioneer spirit, though, was never exclusively Anglo in attitude. America is, of course, more than a single region or state, more than a single colony or ethnic group. Country, in fact, encompasses the pioneer spirit as expressed through myriad ethnic points of reference.

As America was settled and immigrants gravitated to specific areas of the country, their relatives tended to join them. Thus they perpetuated and preserved ideals and traditions that had sustained and given them strength. Like the earliest settlers, new pioneers translated their skills to new climates, new materials, and their new lifestyle. As these waves of people were assimilated into America's lifestyle, they integrated the textures, colors, and patterns of beloved objects from their native heritage into their new American country homestyle.

When people from other nations look to America and to Americans, they describe this land—these people—in words that reflect the Country way of life: Welcoming . . . Inviting . . . Friendly . . . Generous . . . Energetic . . . Daring . . . Wholesome . . . Forthright . . . Humorous . . .

These words fuse into the spirit that inspired and guided our ancestors and our forefathers. These are the words that, generation after generation, drew immigrants to our shores. These are the words that shaped America and made it a place where anyone and everyone could believe in themselves, and could feel free to find a place to call home.

Many of our ancestors arrived on the shores of this nation as escape: escape from persecution; escape from famine; escape from poverty; escape from terror. They

came, wave upon wave of them, in search of freedom, believing that here, in America, anything was possible. Here, in America, they would be independent, find a better life. Here they would be sheltered. Here they could make a home.

They came, for the most part, with few possessions but many ideas—and one shared Dream: Life in the New World had to be better than that in the Old.

Four hundred years ago, when the very first settlers arrived, America, of course, was not a tamed environment. The land those settlers confronted was big and wild and, in many ways, quite terrible. Life was harsh. Forests had to be cleared; trees had to be felled; stones and roots had to be wrenched from the earth. But the Dream sustained them: They would live where they wanted to live. They would live how they wanted to live. They would make a home in this land.

The American home was born as a compact bastion or defense against wilderness and weather. At the outset, home was nothing more than a single room comprising four walls and a roof, perhaps a chimney and an earth floor. The entire life of the family took place in this cramped space. Amenities were few; furnishings crude. There was no time for play.

Soon enough, however, skills from abroad translated to good use in the new land. More than anything, those early colonists wanted to emulate their European forebears. They wanted homes that were comfortable and possessions that—if they could not be imported—could simulate those left behind. They wanted, in short, to show off their new and hard-won prosperity. By the time of the American Revolution, in fact, seven generations of colonists had spread over the Eastern seaboard and were moving westward. Travel back and forth across the ocean was not uncommon, and people such as Thomas Jefferson who were instrumental in designing an American Constitution and government were, quite literally, designing the American home as well.

By the Revolution, indeed, there was an inbred hierarchy: architecture and design reflected levels of wealth and status.

The American home had already evolved from one room to two, these flanking a chimney to capitalize on its warmth. Two rooms doubled to four, and with the addition of a second story, doubled again to eight. The new center hall staircase anchored the house, and the various rooms responded to functional needs—for entertaining, for cooking, for sleeping. Regional variations on the center chimney and center hall colonial-style houses emerged, too, and specialized zones such as pantries and outdoor porches increased the flexibility of the living spaces. Now, the home was—to the new rich—no longer a symbol of survival but a symbol of status.

The furnishings necessary to decorate these houses were no longer simple, rugged, or of necessity multi-purpose. American craftsmen and cabinetmakers responded to the demand for beautiful furnishings by creating new and unique masterpieces. For their masterpieces, though, as for architectural ornament, craftsmen looked to European models for inspiration. Chippendale, Sheraton, and Hepplewhite all translated to American design, as distilled through the best that was seen in London or imported from England, conduit to the Colonies. Boston, Newport, Philadelphia, and Charleston all produced cabinetmakers of substantial talent. And, against the surround of fine architecture and furniture, imported fabrics, porcelains, and other objects went on display.

These accoutrements, of course, marked the homestyle of the elite. History books look to this elite, the American aristocracy, as the creators of America.

The Bicentennial of 1976, celebrating the two hundredth birthday of the Declaration of Independence, refueled a passion for all things American, and a re-evaluation of Americana. But at that moment, the focus was still on the America of that elite. The America of the Bicentennial looked back to the best, and evoked a heritage based, in the main, on Anglo-American roots—and designs from the original Thirteen Colonies. Attention focused on the finest antiques, the most exquisite crafts. Williamsburg, sponsored by the Rockefellers; Winterthur by Henry Francis DuPont; the Shelburne Museum of Electra Havemeyer Webb and Greenfield Village of Henry Ford were recognized as collections of immeasurable quality—but, indeed, these also attested to an eye for the finest as acquired by the very rich. What of the pioneer? The simple, the rustic, the rugged?

Country decorating absorbs all these various influences. Scandinavian and Austrian painted furnishings, embellished with pretty floral motifs, take their place beside rustic American painted furniture exhibiting worn layers of milk paint. Finnish baskets cluster alongside Indian baskets, or Shaker baskets, or Nantucket lightship baskets. Italian and French faience pottery can be grouped with white ironstone. Portuguese painted ceramic tiles can be interspersed with Mexican terracotta pavers. The intermingling of furnishings and accessories, both antique and not-so-old, energizes the Country style and gives it resonance and depth.

Ethnic handicrafts tie in with ethnic traditions and are a visible example of connections with family and community, ritual and ceremony. All speak of a freedom of expression and individuality that personalize a home. The meticulous stitchery of a Polish homily, for instance, not only embellishes a piece of needlework, but also serves as a reminder of great-grandparents who communicate the saying to their offspring. The sinuous form of a clay *santo* recreates a religious image drawn from rituals repeated throughout generations of Hispanic ceremonies. Geometric motifs woven into a Navaho blanket speak volumes about myths and beliefs inherited from Indian ancestors in the American Southwest. A particular form of glaze on a lovingly hand-formed pot carries on a Japanese kinship with pottery.

Country decorating, and country crafts, in honoring individual expression within the context of American design, describe a most democratic homestyle. Country's embrace is warm and welcoming; everything in the country-style setting carries equal weight and is of equal importance to the appearance of the house as a whole.

The Country look in decorating is not only democratic, it is many-layered, welcoming materials and goods from many periods, and pieces both old and new. Classic country furnishings, those cherished for their rustic appeal, are in fact, not particularly old; many date only from the nineteenth and early twentieth centuries. Contrived for utilitarian reasons, these pieces were made to be used daily, not simply to be admired.

Some collectors of country, however, want to mingle and display finer-quality heirlooms associated

with particular cabinetmakers and designs with their less formal pieces. As American furnishings and objects have escalated in value over the past decade, collectors dare mix pieces from various periods, and many seek rarer and rarer examples of authentic American designs from every period. A classic American Windsor chair, for example, or a highboy, or a huntboard is eagerly sought after by those who can afford it.

On the other hand, because of the scarcity of upholstered furnishings and beds dating from long ago, many collectors of country are integrating fine-quality reproductions into their room schemes. Aided and abetted by museum programs, collectors can round out furnishings with line-for-line copies of authentic designs, or adaptions that make concessions to contemporary comfort without sacrificing attention to detail and overall design. A newly-made Queen Anne-style wing chair, for instance, or a pencil-post bed, or a camelback sofa, tend to be scaled somewhat larger than their eighteenth-century antecedents because people today, who will live with these pieces, are generally taller and heavier than our colonial ancestors.

Fine reproduction fabrics and wallcoverings, especially-mixed paints, and authentically-detailed lighting fixtures and rugs all complement the country look by bringing to the marketplace adaptations of beloved objects that no longer exist in abundance. These, too, cater to twentieth-century needs; a chandelier, for example, may be electrified; a wallcovering may be coated with vinyl so that it can be cleaned easily.

Some reproductions are manufactured in quantity and are available nationwide; other designs are custom-made by artists and craftspeople who have chosen to work selectively on the few types of furniture or accessories they love the best. Studios and ateliers respond to the demand for their almost-one-of-a-kind objects by working on an intimate scale, either on their own, or with a few assistants or partners. Their wares, many signed and numbered, bequeath a legacy that links them to generations of craftspeople and cabinetmakers: that the object has been formed, meticulously, by hand.

Hands-on is one term that characterizes country decorating; the country-style room is warm, cozy, friendly, intimate. This intimacy is often reaffirmed in personal handicraft, a personal involvement in the decorative touches and accents that give a room its unique appeal. Back in the seventeenth and early eighteenth centuries, for example, before wallpapers became available, walls might be embellished with stenciled decorations. Today, stenciling is one technique that can be employed quickly and easily, without special instruction, to recall colonial designs and lend an air of authenticity to a period room. Stenciling, too, can be applied to fabric or furniture as well as to walls or floors. Stenciling is the most flexible of crafts because single motifs can be combined effortlessly to make a personal statement.

Home sewing techniques, too, can easily reproduce colonial designs. A simple gathered curtain or bed hanging, for instance, can be readily run up on the sewing machine. Cross-stitch, cable stitch, and backstitch, embroidered over traced patterns on graceful linens, translate even the simplest fabrications into family heirlooms. Crafts such as quilting that typically require more patience and expertise can also be accomplished with the help of the sewing machine.

Many crafts are convivial. Sharing the experience of stenciling a wall, making an herbal wreath, or painting a floorcloth is, like the quilting bee of colonial times, a way of getting together with friends. Many craftspeople who turn professional, in fact, enjoy working under the auspices of a crafts cooperative. Some come together at country fairs and shows to display their wares and, in the tradition of itinerant craftsmen of earlier times, to share stories and information.

Country fairs and antiques shows are forums for the serious collector as well as for craftspeople. Antique accessories, to almost everyone who enjoys country decorating, not only complement but validate the country room. The reference to history, and historical associations, are still more links of yesterday to today and generation to generation. The joy of collecting is infectious . . . rummaging through flea markets, bidding at an auction; discovering a country dealer with similar interests and passions often becomes part of a family heritage. The adventure of collecting is more fun when shared, especially between generations.

Country collections are far-reaching. From samplers stitched up by young women learning both their alphabet and needlework techniques to simple kitchen utensils that perform utilitarian tasks, collections capture heart and soul. Special collections may be acquired just for display; others might be assembled purely for everyday use, to continue a tradition of joyful function and family services.

The collector may concentrate on a single collectible, such as baskets, or indulge a passion for all things with a country flavor. Whatever one's personal taste or bias, any collection brings texture, color, and individuality to the country setting.

Although the collector may be serious about collecting, and although a collection may be serious in itself, once a room or house takes itself too seriously, it loses the air of informality and generosity that coincides with the country spirit, and the room loses its life.

For country decorating, at heart, is full of life, full of love, and full of joy. The country room is totally accepting; it will gracefully change or evolve to include new and wonderful collections or crafts.

Country—country living and country decorating— is a continuum. As a way of life and a way of living, it has endured for almost four hundred years because, above all and after all, Country is about connections: connections to generations past and connections to generations yet to come. Country links grandparent to parent and parent to child. Country links friend to friend. Country makes friends of strangers and family of friends. Country reaffirms and reinforces bonds of camaraderie and kinship.

The love of Country grew out of sharing. The love of Country grew out of caring. And love of Country grew, and grows still, out of love for country—for home, for land and for America.

Living the
COUNTRY
Life

Country Living Rooms

Ten people asked to define the living room would probably describe ten very different environments, for the living room is many things to many people. In a large house, a living room may take on the "caution, do not touch" aura of a parlor. Reserved for special occasions, its decor and furnishings will reflect this elevated role and include many country heirlooms and the family's most treasured antiques. In a smaller house, the living room is more likely to be a typical family room: a versatile place ready for anything from a children's party to an impromptu meal. In style, it would be much less imposing, expressing the relaxed and easygoing spirit of regular use.

The country-style living room seeks to be a comfortable, sociable environment. Formal and informal elements meet here and blend into one seamless whole: fine china or crystal can coexist with colorful folk art, family photographs, or perhaps an idiosyncratic display of sentimental value-only mementoes. Even when consciously simulating a classic setting, it would hardly suit to set up a barricade of rigid seating and then expect anyone to remain for long. So upholstered pieces with a classic profile, such as a camelback settee or high back wing chair, are plumped out and softened with extra padding or pillows, quilts, and throws for greater comfort. The fabrics may be documentary designs reproduced from patterns in museum collections; simple homespun checks, plaids, or stripes; or flowery polished cottons. Fragile pieces can be showcased in ways that highlight them, but still keep them out of reach. Bookcases, mantels, and wall niches provide stylish safety; tabletops, by contrast, prefer collectibles and cherished objects that beg to be handled.

Log Living Rooms

America's log cabins, with their muscular simplicity so reminiscent of the pioneer spirit, have grown up. The warmth of their wood still fosters a feeling of security and solidity, but today's log cabins have been leavened with an abundance of natural light. Sun streams in through skylights and windows that are kept bare or perhaps draped with lace. Logs may be pale or bleached; floors left light or dressed with softly colored rugs. Furniture can be more delicately proportioned, and slipcovers may blush with cabbage roses.

One-Room Living

Certain country interiors lend themselves wonderfully to studio or one-room living. Intimacy is achieved by creating activity "islands" for relaxing, dining, and working on a loom, within the space. In such a large area, the primary colors of handmade quilts add punch and drama.

The whitewashed barn, top, was designed strictly for guests. In place of standard fabrics, sheeting has been used for easy care.

A trompe l'oeil wood stove and wall of plates set the stage for this light-hearted room, above. Striped fabric unifies both areas.

Antique Rugs

Handmade and highly individual, antique rugs were created from snippets and scraps of fabric. Lightweight cottons and linens were woven into rag rugs; sturdy wools were braided and sewn into rounds or ovals. Hooked rugs, of fabric strips pulled through a burlap-type backing, encouraged great freedom of expression with floral, geometric, and elaborate scenic designs, as the rug maker did not have to be concerned with a long warp and woof but could easily change colors from scrap to scrap.

Finished hooked rugs were often so prized that they covered a table or bed rather than the floor. The popularity of these rugs has only increased, and today many of the finest are considered art. The smallest ones can be set on tabletops or dressers; larger rugs may be given prominent floor space or even be mounted and hung on walls.

Braided rugs display great richness, with colors and hues modulating from strand to strand, ring to ring. When set on the floor, hooked rugs were often flopped to preserve their faces from wear, and then upended when company came.

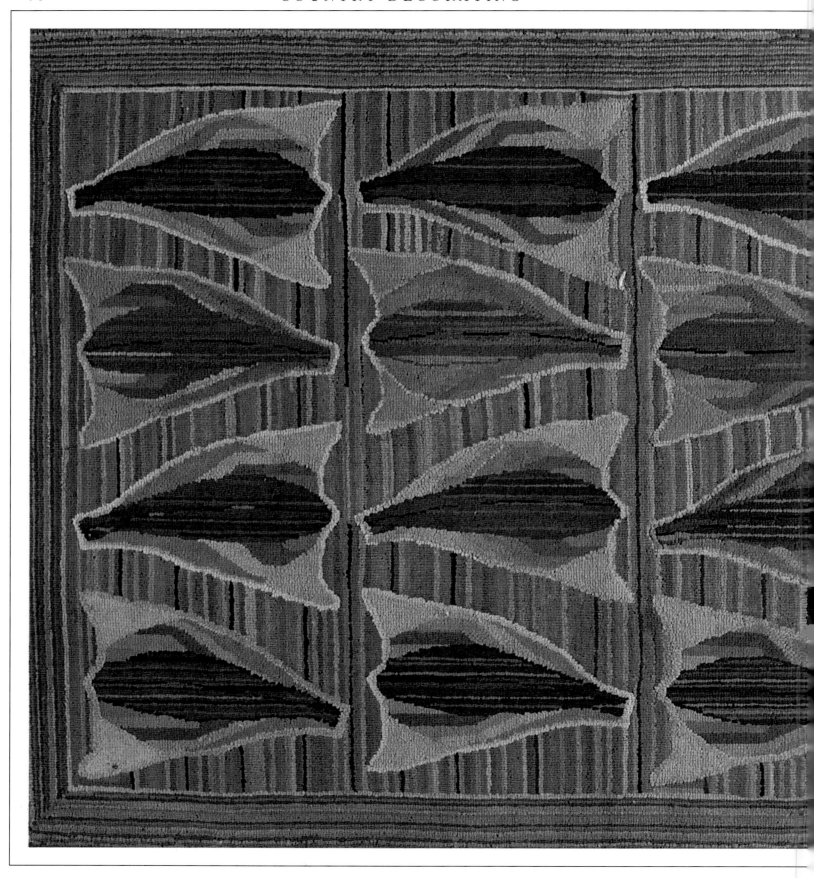

*T*hese hooked rugs are called "Grenfell" rugs, for the English missionary Dr. Wilfred Grenfell, who helped the rug makers of Labrador, Newfoundland, turn their home craft into saleable art. Made between 1911 and 1940, Grenfell rugs usually depict scenes from local life, like the polar bears, igloo, and cod fillets.

The Colorful Living Room

Through color, a living room is made to feel intimate or expansive, lively or calm; as bright colors stir conversation, soft shades encourage tranquility. Color controls both the mood of the room and how it actually looks. Dark tones advance and light ones recede, and deftly applied paint can visually draw in or expand a space, transforming a room for a relatively small investment of time or money.

White, of course, is the most amplifying color, or non-color, for it renders walls virtually invisible. In a white room, everything stands out against the neutral ground, and textures seem especially pronounced. Conversely, a burgundy or other deep-toned room will tend to blur architectural distinctions, so that the furnishings themselves come more into focus. Against a dark backdrop, furniture needs equally intense color or pattern to hold its identity. Pattern, in fact, is more assertive than texture in colorful rooms.

Given the primary role of color in a room, it is advisable to choose a palette after considering furnishings and, particularly, available light. Color changes dramatically in different light, and what appears pale or friendly in a sunlit south-facing room looks cool and darker in northern or fluorescent light.

Scientific analysis shows that early Colonists actually had brighter colors than we thought. Realizing the psychological importance of color, they believed their palette was an antidote to dreary weather. Colonial red, in fact, was truly invigorating. By contrast, heather green, below, soothes and pacifies. White, left, can be anything to anyone; texture and pattern determine the mood it inspires.

Advertising Art

Americans have always advertised—household goods, health remedies, politicians, and get-rich-quick schemes. One of the earliest tradesman's signs, the striped barber's pole was an ad for the minor surgery that barbers once performed. Another popular tradesman's symbol, carved wood Indians began to appear outside tobacco shops in the last half of the nineteenth century. Few have survived from that era, and authentic examples are greatly sought after.

In the nineteenth century, bold colorful graphics were wed to advertising on packaging and later to product "giveaways," complimentary items that, in the days before radio and TV, were the manufacturer's best means of gaining name recognition. Ads were emblazoned on everything from calendars and cards to pocket mirrors, trays, and lapel pins, as well as on the products themselves. Today, many of these items are popular collectibles for their graphic qualities as much as for the nostalgia they evoke.

Colorful tins and canisters held household staples—anything from stove polish to soap flakes. Larger canisters contained as much as half a year's supply of basics such as coffee, tea, or biscuits. Once the product had been consumed, the tin could be filled over and over, becoming an enduring reminder of the advertiser's product. Novelty tins in the shapes of cars, trains, and boats would have a second, more demanding life as toys, which has made them rare and much sought after.

*C*olorful displays such as this covered wagon dating from the earlier part of this century, top left, are especially collectible examples of advertising art.

*T*he ingenious and industrious Shakers were neither reticent nor unimaginative about advertising their goods. Taking advantage of a reputation for impeccable workmanship, they virtually mass-produced product packages, unlike their scarcer furniture. Today Shaker seed boxes are coveted almost as much as Shaker furnishings and accessories. Simple graphic box labels, left, are at once declamatory and somehow sweetly nostalgic. A collection of old tins, right, displays one appeal of advertising art: typographic expertise.

Casual Living Rooms

A favorite country setting, the casual living room is a relaxed, easygoing place designed with comfort in mind. Country casual takes its mood from big, soft sofas dressed with plenty of pillows; scattered throughout, baskets are filled with cheery flowering plants, cozy lap rugs, or magazines to leaf through. Clear colors such as rose pink, sky blue, buttercup yellow, and alabaster white harmonize. Family keepsakes are displayed on open shelves, together with books, folk art, framed photographs, and bowls of potpourri, in a constantly evolving collage of colors and shapes.

Interesting arrangements juxtapose varied colors, textures, and forms. A single quilt, above, or a collection of hooked rugs, left, beckons the eye. Outdoor elements— a clutch of field flowers, a tray of pine cones—instill freshness. Disparate items can be combined: gameboards, painted cows, hand tools, and a kerosene lamp.

The Wing Chair

oward the end of the seventeenth century, the wing chair—or "easie chair"—made its way from the Continent to England and then to the Colonies. It has persisted as the single most popular style of upholstered furniture in the house. And for good reason: its amply padded side pieces, or wings, shelter its occupant from drafts, and when the chair is drawn close to the hearth, retain warmth within its recess.

Over the years, its details have changed to reflect prevailing fashions. In the early eighteenth century, for example, wing chairs had the curvaceous cabriole leg terminating in the pad foot of contemporary Queen Anne furniture. Its wings and arms, too, flowed in a continuous graceful line, a hallmark of Queen Anne design. In contrast, in later styles such as the Sheraton and Hepplewhite, the wings rested atop the arms.

Wing chairs come in all sizes. The narrowest, with mere slivers of wings, are called "host chairs," as they are designed to stand at the head of the dining table. Some massive wing chairs approximate the loveseat in bulk and, in fact, may seat two. An early English version of the wing chair tipped back, via a ratchet mechanism, for sleeping; many of today's recliners emulate these distant forebears, wings and all.

In a summery room, far left, a pair of delicate wing chairs in a sprightly floral chintz is comfortable in an informal setting. The scroll-arm wing chair with flame-stitch upholstery shares a cozy hearthside with two other favorites: a deep blue camelback settee and a highback settle bench, left. The three surround a trundle bed that the owner converted into a coffee table by placing glass across the rope mattress supports.

This contemporary wing chair, right, epitomizes the essential appeal of classic design.

The Shaker Legacy

"**P**ut your hands to work and your hearts to God," admonished Mother Ann, founder of the Shaker sect. Dedicating their lives to order, cleanliness, and worship, Shakers were expected to work for the common good, each according to his or her individual expertise. Striving for self-sufficiency, Shakers made as many of their necessities as possible, bestowing their craftsmanship upon even the humblest household items.

Renowned for the fine quality of their workmanship and for their ingenuity, Shakers are often credited with the invention and/or the perfection of the flat broom and the clothes pin; they were among the first to make rocking chairs for the general populace. In their concern for practicality, Shakers either built-in furniture or raised it high off the floor so a broom could easily pass underneath. They spaced pegs across the walls so that every object that could hang would, even chairs.

The majority of Shaker furniture was made during the nineteenth century, at a time when mainstream styles often ran to the elaborate. In contrast, the Shaker idea of beauty was based on function, and their work exhibits a craftsmanship that is rarely surpassed. The scarcity and popularity of Shaker furniture have moved it beyond most people's means, but Shaker-inspired design retains the timelessness that makes it sublimely appropriate to a country setting.

A set of twelve "tilter" chairs, whose Shaker-invented ball and socket allowed their occupants to lean back, flanks a long dining table.

This triple-slat armless chair with a woven seat is a standard still emulated in contemporary reproductions.

The Shaker communities scattered throughout the East and Midwest chose similar design motifs, but added their own subtle signatures. Finials on chairs, for instance, differed slightly from community to community. Nesting oval pantry boxes with distinctive finger joints and a collapsible table swift for winding yarn were popular items sold to the outside world.

Shakers created tiny versions of their simple cloaks and bonnets to sell as dolls' clothing.

Country in the City

Many city dwellers have roots in the country, and have found that living in a high-rise, townhouse, tenement, or garden apartment does not mean having to forsake country graces. Yes, city spaces often do lack architectural distinction or that lovely patina of age, but the boxy white room can be a perfect foil for the country look.

Indeed, the very spareness of a typical city apartment heightens the sensuous impression and warmth of rustic textures, colors, and patterns. The more ambitious country approach is to opt for architectural embellishments such as ceiling beams or Shaker-style pegboards to lend authenticity to the surroundings. Simple touches, though, can speak volumes: shutters at the window or a stenciled border bring freshness to a room. A hand-rubbed pale wood mantelpiece, pickled floors, and a friendly palette will all contribute to a country feeling. The easiest solution of all is to create a surrounding of country elements, relying on flowers, baskets, quilts, linens and laces, or perhaps a favorite collection of anything with a "downhome" flavor, with simple wicker or pine furniture.

Pale striped sofas face off across a farm table cut down to coffee table height, above. The new cupboard, Shaker-like in its austerity, shelters a stereo and television. The oxidized weathervane is a collector's treasure.

Hand-painted pastel fabrics envelop the overstuffed seating in a townhouse living room, left. A damaged quilt was salvaged to create slipcovers for the twig settee, while a coffee table made from gnarled driftwood continues the sun bleached look.

Beautifully weathered blue-painted furnishings are the hallmarks of this rental apartment. The impact of the steer skull, a souvenir of the Southwest, is softened by pairing it with a spatterware jug of tulips.

*G*ood country anti-
dotes to hectic city living: *A*
frugal tenement living room,
top left, is overfurnished to
become cozy, not cramped.
Bouquets of roses casually
strung from the mantel fill
the room with scent as they
air dry. A collection of
majolica and a hooked rug
echo the room's soft, rosy
hue. In an elegant prewar
apartment, below left, the
soothing color scheme is
echoed in peonies splashed
over linen slipcovers, window
valances, and a fireboard.
The soapstone mantel was
painted to accentuate its relief
carvings.

*T*he focal point of a
standard high-rise apart-
ment, top right, is a working
fireplace. Pale sofas flank
the hearth, and the orange
and white quilt warms the
room. To make every inch of
space count, the owner of a
modern one-bedroom flat,
below, subdivided it to create
an extra bedroom. A shuttered
window peers into the new
room; to "age" them, the
shutters were hand-rubbed with
milk paint. A striking buffalo
plaid fabric invites lounging
on a cozy banquette; storage
is concealed underneath.

Displaying Collections

The rule of thumb for any display is to maintain scale and balance. Baskets and stoneware, for example, coexist compatibly, above, because of their similar tone and line.

One object is considered an accessory; two constitute the beginning of a collection. Collections may be composed of one thing—quilts, baskets, a style of pottery—or a jumble of disparate objects that reflect personal taste. Once a collection begins to accumulate, though, where does it go? Country decorating, in fact, relies heavily on the art of arranging, and collections often lie at the heart of successful country homes.

Some collections, due to their rarity and fragility, should be contained, and deserve display in a glass cabinet or similar protected environment. Others, more rugged, can be moved around and serve as mobile decorative accents. Indeed, many American wares were created originally for utilitarian purposes so that continued use enhances their intrinsic merit and only adds to their lustre. When pressed into service again, a yellowware pie plate, for instance, or a patchwork quilt, reaffirms its connection with its—and our—past.

As it evolves, a collection may become greater than the sum of its parts. These miniature houses, gathered across the mantel, look like a quaint village.

Decoys

Early decoys resembled their prey only in size and silhouette; not until the 1840s did they evolve into meticulous recreations of specific species. Most commonly they were carved from cedar or white juniper, but decoys could be made from whatever was at hand, even old driftwood. Predictably the results were highly individualistic and varied, including "stick-ups" and "flatties," two-dimensional decoys of land or shore birds that were not designed to float. Some dedicated makers attached real feathers to their decoys. Since wildfowl follow predetermined migratory routes, regional decoys mimic regional wildfowl. Local variations in the style of carving abound: those from Stratford, Connecticut, Cape Cod, and the Delaware River area are the most well-known.

Floating decoys were augmented with ballast and anchor to make them stay put. Those not released in water, such as shore bird decoys, stood on an artificial "leg." For this home display, the legs have been anchored to pedestals and perched atop a cupboard shelf. New decoys tend to be molded of cork or fiberglass. New and old are equally collectible and will share a cupboard in complete harmony.

A gaggle of geese swim across specially designed shelves, left. Some decoys boast moveable necks and heads; others, more artistic, turn their heads in naturalistic poses. A swan, for instance, tucks her head under her wing, and a Canadian goose arches his neck in a hiss of self-defense. Decoys were sometimes fashioned of canvas stretched taut over a wire armature, so that they would be lighter and more bouyant than their wooden counterparts.

Table Displays

Image scale and intent, what is placed upon a tabletop
is more intimate and telling of personal style than
the surrounding furniture, fabric, or wallcovering. Family
photographs, heirlooms, fresh flowers, or small collections reflect their owner's fondest fancies.

Whimsically juxtaposed, the elements in a table-
scape complement a room, and can be changed and
adapted more readily than large furnishings. Combining
framed pictures, keepsakes, a vacation souvenir, or a
favorite piece of pottery or trinket with bowls of fresh
fruits and flowers and new table linens shows a freedom
of arrangement that hanging paintings or assembling
cased collections does not. This kind of still-life, though,
must be allowed to "breathe": too much clutter stifles
a table—and our enjoyment of it.

Above, colorful spools of yarn in a basket are an unexpected addition to the cozy coffee table display.

*F*resh flowers and scented potpourri, below, bring several small table scenes to life instantly. Glowing under a fringed lampshade, a delicate water-color rests flat upon a floral chintz tablecloth, right.

Rose-dappled cushions, right, each subtly different, are piled onto white wicker to bring summer to this room. Great bouquets of real roses repeat the pastel floral theme. A lush mélange of cushioned wicker, lace, and Victorian silver creates the inviting mood of this room, below. For evenings, an Art Nouveau torchiere radiates atmospheric lamplight.

Placed between two windows, top right, this fainting couch encourages daydreams, reminiscences, and afternoon naps. The stenciled frieze pattern was inspired by the local Carolina Lily.

Ruffled rosy pillows and window valances give this sunlit living room the mood of a year-round porch, far right. An Irish pine cupboard houses quilts and antique pottery. The petite drop leaf table is set for dolls' tea.

Summer Living Rooms 63

Summer Living Rooms

For the Victorians, living rooms were subdued formal places densely layered with heavy dark fabrics and encrusted with ornaments. Overladen with gewgaws, they were often oppressive and airless. Today, living rooms have become lighter in spirit. In summer, especially, the living room may completely give itself over to the mood of the season. Stripped of winter's heavier colors, scented with a heady mix of garden flowers, the summer room is wonderfully evocative. Dreamy, tranquil, and tenderly cosseting, such rooms conjur up summer thoughts simply by association. Diaphanous window dressings cajole breezes indoors; lace and linens soften hard edges. The delicate tracery of wicker especially suits the summer living room, and warm pastel-covered walls will cast an appealing glow, like late afternoon sunlight, rendering the setting irresistible.

Antique Linens

The most exquisite linens, whether chastely plain or painstakingly embellished with lace, open cut-work, embroidery, or monograms, were often created for a bridal trousseau. Young women, as prescribed by the etiquette of the day, amassed dozens of bed and table linens. All too often, however, these languished in a trunk because they were presumed too fragile and too precious for everyday use. Today, antique linens, many untouched, are emerging from trunk, attic, and armoire to be cherished and used on a daily basis. Rare and costly linens, of course, still require discretionary handling, but utilitarian ones are finding their rightful place all over the home.

Many highly-prized linens were crafted in Europe during the Victorian era; these often differ in size from those made in the States. European bed linens, for example, tended to be much longer as the top sheet was customarily folded farther down over the bed. Table napkins, too, were larger, to completely cover the lap. Specialized linens include bureau scarves, antimacassars and shams, and doilies, devised to complement accessories such as tea trays and muffineers.

A handful of mismatched linen napkins and hankies has found new life as shelf liners, left.

Recently salvaged, a strip of crochet-fringed linen underscores an open shelf, top.

Simple linen cloths are loosely draped over a bedroom sofa; others are displayed as naive art.

Folk Art

Connoisseurs define folk art in strict terms: objects of artistic merit created purely for decorative purposes. With its often religious or ethnic origins, folk art, even when anonymous, is unique and expresses an individual sensibility. Crafts—rugs, baskets, pottery—are conceived with a function in mind and are often produced in multiples. They represent the good old-fashioned virtues of durability and hard work. Folk art, on the other hand, harbors mystery and an intense inner meaning, be it sober or whimsical.

Folk art, though, appeals to collectors for many of the same reasons as do crafts: because of its naiveté, honesty, and vernacular charm. Some functional objects, considered crafts at first, have been elevated to the status of folk art as their artistic merit was perceived. The quilt, for instance, has dramatically appreciated in stature and value, and is now deemed folk art. Folk art, like fine art, is cherished on an intellectual and an emotional level.

Animals, especially those associated with home and farm, have inspired artisans for generations. San Ysidro, top left, is the patron saint of farmers in Spanish-speaking countries, and in the American Southwest he is held in high esteem. Noah's ark, opposite bottom, tells a story in three dimensions, and its implicit moral could be quietly reinforced in child's play. Barnyard beasts are particularly appealing subjects that are both whimsical and graphic. The wooden cows, left, and the smiling dog, below, illustrate the fine balance folk art objects strike between the serious and the humorous.

Symbolic totems such as the heart-in-hand, below, calmed superstitious spirits as well as proferred welcome.

*A bridal box from
Switzerland, above, would
have been carried from the
maiden's home to her new
residence. Pull toys such as
the horse with a real horse-
hair tail were once com-
monplace playthings. Horses,
like the rocking horse, left,
are collected now as art objects
rather than as toys. Weathervanes, including the Indian
reproduction, right, were
crafted to be seen from a
distance, as they revolved in
the wind.*

Country Dining Rooms

Of all the functions assigned to the various rooms of the house, dining—or eating—is the most mobile. Dining can occur anywhere a table and chairs and food are set up. If the dining room per se has been rendered virtually obsolete in many contemporary home designs, it is still perceived as highly desirable by people who equate a separate dining area with a more gracious and hospitable lifestyle.

In the country-style house, a separate dining room may be a ceremonial place, set aside for Sunday dinners, celebrations of birthdays and other family milestones, and holiday feasts. But dining need not be a ritual; nibbling snacks or eating a light lunch, for instance, is certainly dining. So, because the art of dining complements the act of cooking, very often eating in or near the kitchen suits country living.

In any dining area, the table and chairs form the nucleus of the design scheme. Whether rugged or polished, plain or padded, the chairs should be comfortable. The size and shape of the table also contribute to the mood of the room. A circular table, for example, where diners face each other, tends to be less formal. Lighting is important and should be versatile enough for any occasion from a sunny tea time to a dinner party glittering with candlelight. Linens and serving pieces regarded as cherished heirlooms can be brought to the table on special occasions or, if truly loved, set out daily. Sterling silver, for example, simply looks better and better the more it is handled.

Above all, country dining encourages improvisation ... beautiful vegetables from the garden, fresh-baked breads, and just-cut blooms from the flower bed are all tempting elements for a centerpiece or room decoration. Favorite collectibles or prized examples of folk art may highlight a tabletop too. There is really only one rule: that hospitality be the guide.

The Keeping Room

Rustically appointed keeping rooms vividly recapture the atmosphere of colonial days, and the bigger the hearth the better. A spartan daybed, above, is drawn up to the hearth to take advantage of its warmth in this keeping room. A triple-strip rug outlines a dining area in a sparely-furnished keeping room, right. Baskets parade across a huge hand-hewn support beam stretching over a scrub-top kitchen table. Traditional six-panel doors flanking the fireplace lead, respectively, to the front of the house and to the basement.

The keeping room—part kitchen, part living room, part bedroom, part workshop—was America's earliest general room. All domestic activity centered around the hearth, which was both the sole heat source and the site of all food preparation. As Americans built larger houses, the cooking hearth was turned to the back of the house, to a kitchen separate from the rest of the home. Today's eat-in kitchen, with its informal seating area, is really an outgrowth of the keeping room.

Ironically, in a modern home the keeping room now has become a luxury, affordable only to the homeowner who has a spare room with a fireplace or wood stove. When anchored by a long scrubbed table set before the hearth and furnished with any variety of rustic antiques, the keeping room nostalgically evokes the colonial "heart of the home." In an authentic keeping room, in fact, there would be no intrusion of the twentieth century. But television and microwave can consort with baskets, candles, and drying herbs. Everyone gravitates to this room, less from necessity, than by choice.

Checks bold and petite and stripes thick and narrow create a harmony of blues on these pages. Stacking homespuns protects them from deterioration caused by the sun and reinforces the vitality of their patterns and tones. Blues from pale to deepest indigo can harmonize in a more satisfying way than any other color. Collected in a cupboard, the checks and plaids set up a counterbalance to the boxy outlines of their enclosure — windowpane to windowpane, as it were. Near right, the vibrant colors of Amish rag balls vividly contrast with linear blue homespuns.

Homespuns

During the eighteenth and early nineteenth centuries, linen and cotton, and occasionally wool fibers were spun at home into plain-weave fabrics for bedding, bolster cases, feather bed tickings, kerchiefs, tablecloths, and clothing. Homespun fabric endears itself to collectors as much for the feel of its natural fibers and its "plain hand" as its unassuming graphic check, stripe, and plaid patterns. The most popular coloring, and today's uncontested favorite too, was indigo blue. Of all the vegetable dyes, indigo—extracted from the indigo and woad plants—was the most readily available,

and it resisted fading and bleeding. Other colors such as brown and yellow were far more difficult to produce and thus are rarer. Handwoven fabrics generally have a more irregular selvage, or side finish, than their factory-woven imitators.

Reproduction homespuns, simulating their forebears in texture and hue, adapt well to large-scale decorating projects such as bedhangings, tablecloths, and curtains, as they are wider than most standard fabrics. Many new homespuns are designed to complement older cloth.

Formal Dining Rooms

Like the parlor, in earlier times the formal dining room was reserved for visitors, solemn occasions, and Sunday dinner. The term "formal," in other words, became synonymous with restraint and elegance. Today, though, formal may embrace any setting that respects and dignifies its furnishings, and by implication, its guests. The art of entertaining in a formal setting with one's best tableware, food, and drink is simply a careful and caring effort to create a special occasion. In such an atmosphere, a return to ritual and manners matters, and

these days, even if the best is simple and rustic, that is as important to success as the occasion itself.

In contrast to more casual rooms, formal often follows custom; in terms of taste and style, the personal and the idiosyncratic do not play as prominent a role in this setting. Consequently, fabrics and wallcoverings should coordinate, and their colors and patterns, while not necessarily subdued, should be restrained. Furniture in a formal dining room will, like its surroundings, balance comfort with elegance.

Above, upholstery enhances the regal bearing of parsons chairs, yet the fabric's fresh-sprigged pattern subdues them so that their formality is not overbearing.

The China trade supplied fine porcelain to Americans as early as the eighteenth century. A favorite motif bestowed its name upon a particular china: willowware. The willow wallcovering, like most pictorial wallpapers, left, ennobles a dining room; wing chairs have an air of dignity yet are comfortable and relaxing.

Formal needn't mean opulent; it may just as easily have a simple dignity. Here primitive painted furnishings are precisely arranged to reflect their owners' pride.

A clutch of baskets in artful disarray shows the wonderful interplay of tones, textures, and shapes in such a display.

Antique Baskets

At the foot of a bed, below, a trio of baskets reveals basic weaves: four-square, over/under, and radial thin-splint formation.

These baskets were woven by Indians of the eastern United States, who often decorated baskets by dying splints before weaving.

When the first European settlers arrived on these shores, they found a venerable culture rich in crafts. Of these, basket weaving was especially advanced. Indian baskets, woven from thin splints of wood or coiled grasses, sometimes even incorporating feathers or simple painted decorations, display a sophisticated skill and refined sense of design.

Some baskets, such as the bushel, indicate measure. Others' nicknames declare an idiosyncratic profile—like the buttocks basket and the cat's ear basket. Materials and style of weave will often indicate a basket's origins, and its shape will tell of its function. A tobacco basket, for example, is an immense, flat, open-weave rectangle to help the tobacco leaves air-dry; in the home, this shape lends itself to storage of blankets and linens. Baskets for carrying nuts and berries, by contrast, are small and densely woven to preserve the moisture of their harvest. This tight weave makes them good containers for jewelry, buttons, and potpourri as well.

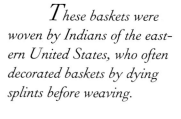

Woodenwares

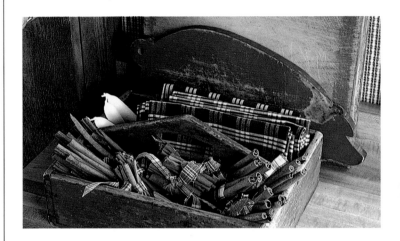

Woodenwares or treen (the Anglo Saxon plural of tree) were once everyday necessities: in the Colonial era, bowls, plates, spoons, cups, spice boxes, scoops, and butter and cookie molds were all made of wood. Wood was plentiful, and unlike metalware, wood household items could be made cheaply and easily by anyone who whittled.

The elegant, sometimes sophisticated styles of woodenware may have been turned on a lathe or carved or whittled by hand. Most commonly they show the amber color and rich texture of the grain of maple, but pine, ash, and birch were also popular woods. Graced only by the natural patterns of grain or burl and by the lustre of use, woodenware is artlessly beautiful.

Many of the containers were based on bucket-like measures. The firken, for example, originated as a barrel of one-quart capacity. For storage, graduated oval boxes were also widely used; of these, the Shaker boxes are only the best-known. Regardless of origin, oval boxes have gone beyond food storage, and are found throughout the house today, filled with magazines, fabrics and yarns, early photographs, or family memorabilia.

Age and use enhance the deep patina of woodenware, but whether utilitarian or merely decorative, a woodenware collection brings its characteristic warmth to any spot.

Knife caddies, candleholders, goblets, mortars and pestles, mashers, and spoons, above, can still be found at flea markets.

Common containers for storing liquids were open-topped; those for dry goods, lidded. The graduated sizes of pantry boxes, right, helped to keep track of the exact quantities of their contents. Most woodenware is unadorned and those with painted finishes are generally more valuable.

A stripped-pine drop leaf table is placed to take advantage of fresh air and garden views, right. Lace-edged embroidered mats dating from the early part of this century mark place settings. On the table, a "spooner" made of faceted glass holds extra flatware.

Informal Dining Rooms

There is something about the sharing and sociability of meals that responds to the informal—a more relaxed, congenial attitude very often seems to enhance the enjoyment of food and company. In many country homes today, informal dining may be set in the kitchen, but often it will take place in a keeping room or breakfast nook, or even outdoors on a porch or patio.

The relaxed atmosphere of informal dining can sometimes be deceptive: it does not mean that the meal has not been thought out or planned. Behind the effortless appearance that helps put guests at ease is some consideration and work. Flair and imagination are also necessary. Informal dinnerware is typically more robust—earthenware or pottery rather than porcelain—and its designs are either painted freehand or at least less studied in composition. Similarly, flowers are more humble, coming from the roadside or backyard, and simply arranged. In fact, almost anything can be a table decoration: a basket overflowing with fresh fruits or vegetables, a display of dried flowers or grasses—whatever comes to hand. During the meal, serving dishes, water pitchers, and wine bottles are left on the table so that guests feel free to help themselves, in this welcoming, informal spirit.

Rag runners criss-cross under purposely mismatched platters, above.

White wicker, straw hats, and layered table linens enhance a romantic mood.

Pottery & Ceramics

Of all handicrafts, none is more sensuous than pottery. The clay itself, even before it is massaged into shapes, is marvelously slippery and solid to the touch, and once fired holds sinuous as well as straight lines. American clays are legion: red, brown, gray, taupe, and white. A few are fine, but most tend to coarseness; American pottery, therefore, is robust. American pottery, too, has traditionally been designed for utilitarian purposes, and shaped or molded into everyday items such as jugs, plates, cups, and bowls. These objects were meant to be handled constantly (although today, because of their porous nature and because many were coated with a lead glaze, they are generally no longer used for serving food).

The potter's wares were embellished with decorations that were simple and unaffected. Spongeware was daubed with a rag; slipware "trailed" with a creamy toothpaste-like clay drizzled through goose quills; "sgraffito"— from the Italian *sgraffiare*, to scratch—designs were incised into the clay with a sharp tool. The glaze assumed a character of its own, too, darkening or crackling over time.

Collectors find that massing pottery achieves the most dramatic effect. Staggered in rows in a stepback cupboard, parading across a mantle or windowsill, or simply clustered on a tabletop, pieces of pottery grouped together find strength in numbers.

From nineteenth century France, Jaspé, far left, is lively and idiosyncratic: no two pieces are alike.

Reproduction slipware, above, emulates its sophisticated antecedents with decorations of different colored clays.

Yellowware's buff clay, left, formed the base for several types of pottery. On its own or decorated with bands of contrasting color, yellowware has always been popular.

Produced only in very small quantity, the charming and simple designs of the Saturday Evening Girls, above, are now very collectible.

The brilliant colors and bold designs of Gaudy Dutch are unmistakable. Made in England in the first quarter of the nineteenth century, these gaily-colored wares inject vitality into any room.

Also enjoying renewed popularity, hand-painted Dedhamware is characterized by its unique crackled surface. Its distinctive rabbit pattern is probably best-known, although the Massachusetts company produced about sixty designs between 1895 and 1943. Owl, dolphin, and cat motifs, and any plates with a pattern in the center and border are especially collectible.

In 1906, civic-minded Boston matrons began the Saturday Evening Girl's club, to train disadvantaged young women. The pottery was in the Arts and Crafts style, using dark borders to outline repeat designs, and sometimes featured children's motifs.

The white crackled glaze that distinguishes Dedham pottery is achieved by rapid cooling after firing. It is set off by cobalt blue bands, above.

A colorful collection of Gaudy Dutch plates, right, is displayed with salt-glazed stoneware.

*S*toneware was fired at extremely high temperatures and coated with a unique glaze containing salt to make it non-porous. Stoneware interiors were also glazed so that these functional jugs, crocks, bottles, and mugs could hold liquids. Its chunky form and durability made stoneware very popular as everyday storage around the home. Typically beige or gray in color with a naive blue design, stoneware held everything from butter to beans. It still makes attractive and practical containers for pickles and preserves.

Sponge, spatter, stick-spatter, and cut-sponge are cousins in clay as it were, as all these forms of pottery are decorated with color daubed directly onto the piece with a sponge. An inexpensive alternative to porcelains, spongewares were first manufactured during the nineteenth century in England, primarily in Staffordshire, to meet American demand for colorful earthenwares.

British manufacturers were adept at varying color and pattern: blue, red, green, and ochre were common colors, and patterns ranged from densely stippled spatter effects to more delicate open grillwork designs. English spongeware also combined overall patterns with specific cut-sponge motifs such as flowers and stars or hand-painted free-style designs.

American spongeware began to appear around the 1830s, but didn't become prevalent until the latter half of the century. Since very few pieces are marked, they are notoriously difficult to date. In color they are limited to a palette of blue or green on white, or brown, green, and ochre; the simple blue and white utilitarian pieces were generally decorated with overall patterns.

English spatterware, left, exhibits a variety of design motifs such as birds or flowers encircled by fields of the actual spatter. The display of spatterware includes an unusual miniature candlestick. Stick-spatterware, above, features brightly colored leaf and flower patterns.

*T*hree joyful blue pitchers show that sponge patterns vary from open to tight, depending on the whim of the potter.

The Colorful Dining Room

In a dining room, color is designed to enhance one specific function, namely, eating. When people gather to share food and conversation, the room is a backdrop, its role a supporting one. As a background, color should be softer, more subdued, so that the table itself always remains the dominant feature in the room. Since table settings change with food and season, the room's color must also be flexible, harmonizing with the brighter, clearer hues of summer flowers and summer sunlight as well as the warmer tones of autumn sun.

Wood tones and white extend the most neutral embrace and are good choices for households with brightly patterned or colored dinnerware. Both dark and pale shades give food, candlelight, and objects, especially those of porcelain or metal, a lustrous glow. If bright color is selected, it is wise to maintain some sort of separation between its intense hue and the colors of the food. A wooden table or white tablecloth, for example, provides an impartial setting so that the food and background color don't compete.

*W*arm umber unites wood, stenciling, and checker-board in a log dining room, left. Honey tones make the room feel especially cozy. Deep red wallpaper behind a collection of pewter plates, pitchers, and cups highlights its patina. The wallpaper's color is tempered by a fine white print.

A white dining room linking a hall and kitchen is very tiny; the eggshell white allows the three areas to blend seamlessly.

Porches invite easy living and dining: the combination of warm sunlight and fresh air seems to mix naturally with good food. An adobe porch, near right, stays cool and comfortable because its thick walls keep out the day's heat. A skylight casts natural light onto the area, and the informal mood is carried through in the unpainted sawbuck table and mismatched furniture, including a leggy child's chair.

Chip-resistant, bulky white restaurant dinnerware stacked in an open-faced cupboard, left, is ideal for casual meals on a porch.

Pink table and chairs set in a pale blue room create a friendly and relaxed atmosphere on an enclosed porch, far right.

When a porch is glassed-in it can be enjoyed year-round, right. The ribbon windows—six-over-sixes—are replaced by screens during the warmer months to increase cross-ventilation. On the floor, glossy marine deck paint repels spills and is easy to clean.

Country Tables

The country table is always welcoming, presenting the bounty of the garden and countryside to be enjoyed by family and friends. Even at its most formal the settings are relaxed: these are not tables where everything is all of a pattern, set stiffly in precise order. Elements mix and match, type is played against type with a delight in the particular charm of each item. The hearty, simple character of stoneware, for instance, will nicely set off a creamy lace tablecloth. Patterns, on dinnerware or table linens, are combined to lend vigor to the setting.

Flowers and fruit improvise for a centerpiece and to decorate place settings, but really almost anything from the house or garden can be brought in to add interest to the table. Country collections of pottery, evergreen boughs or autumn leaves, pine cones, brightly colored toys, or a single piece of folk art will make an intriguing centerpiece. Antique textiles bring their rich colors, patterns, and textures to the table. In the latter case, it's smart to choose a less valuable fabric in case of a mishap. Alternatively, a piece of glass or acrylic cut to fit the table, or a new cloth layered on top handkerchief-style, will protect a valuable tablecloth from spills and crumbs. With candles and good conversation, all the elements are in place for true country dining.

*A*bstract patterns are foils for each other in the dining area, far left. Wrinkled branches in an overscale urn, comb-painted plates, and an intricate hooked rug laid on the table all follow this abstract theme. Placing the fruit plates off-center on the buffet plates draws attention to the color and texture of the freehand design.

*W*hether by itself or mixed with patterned dishes, white ironstone is a good choice. Special pieces such as these teacups without handles, near left, are a visual treat, and warm the hands as well.

*S*peckled buffet plates defuse the white-on-white emphasis in this table setting, right. Napkins, unfolded to become placemats, all point towards the fruit centerpiece. American pressed glass candlesticks, like the wine glasses, purposely do not match. Queen Anne's lace, plucked from the roadside, has been gathered in a pitcher and threaded into twig napkin rings at each place setting.

Country Kitchens

There are people who consider that the country kitchen should be steeped in antiquity. But it's been a while since the butter churn and icebox were state-of-the-art kitchen equipment. The country kitchen, still guided by respect for hard work and common sense, accomodates the most up-to-date appliances and other technologies in a new blend that reflects the best of the old and the new. It is the traditional approach to kitchen decoration and acknowledgement of its multipurpose importance that give this room country flavor. The kitchen is the place from which the family is nourished, both literally and figuratively; a place where food is stored, meals are made, and family and friends naturally gather. It provides adequate and well considered space for the cook, the canner, the baker, and the hostess, as well as room for eating and talking. Wooden tables and chairs, together with antique furnishings, accessories, and collectibles, personalize the room and prevent the kitchen from feeling laboratory-like.

Country kitchens use earthy, humble materials to counterbalance slick equipment: the cordial natural textures and colors of wood, tile, brick, and stone bespeak the kitchen's unassuming character. Special wood veneers such as barn siding can face cabinetry and appliances, unifying the architecture while lending a rustic appeal. Linking banks of cabinets, open shelving displays favorite collections. Pottery, metalwares, wooden utensils, colorful advertising art, and paper goods are all kitchen-oriented collectibles that look well when massed on shelves. Shelves themselves can be lined with colorful papers or draped with lace-trimmed linens. The rich tones and textures of baskets and the heady scent of drying herbs supply sensory interest. These ingredients, like those in a favorite recipe, add flavor, spice, and substance to a country kitchen.

Rustic Kitchens

A primitive farm table is the anchor in a spare kitchen, opposite. A hefty log "corral" fences in the work area in an open western-style kitchen. Sliced logs form the countertops; a wagon wheel was turned into a chandelier. Nineteenth century French copper molds combine function and beauty, right.

The kitchens most immediately associated with the classic country look are rustic. Rough around the edges, unpretentious and informal, rustic kitchens have evolved naturally from the traditional keeping room. All utilize rugged woods, often oak or pine, as one of their main materials. At its most practical, wood camouflages many minor sins: crooked walls, grease spots, discoloration from moisture. Sealed with polyurethane, wood cleans easily, but even stripped or scuffed wood weathers well, attaining a rubbed patina over time.

Because wood is a natural material, it breathes—expands and contracts—and thus functions as an effective insulator. Stylistically, wood evokes memories of old-fashioned kitchens, whether left completely natural, or painted, pickled, or stained. In the compact kitchen knotty pine unifies the cabinets and the floor. People gravitate toward almost any kitchen, it's true, but the rustic kitchen has an everlasting appeal that is generated by a truly unassuming charm.

*T*his collection of bright green-handled cooking utensils is displayed on the enamel top of an oak Hoosier-type cabinet.

Kitchen Collections

Faience and other earthenwares imported from Europe are assembled on open shelves over a stove.

The kitchen is by inclination a casual place and the hub of many activities, so collectors need not be restrained or cautious when decorating this room. As long as everyday wares—dishes, pots and pans, and kitchen utensils—are organized so that they can perform efficiently, then collections can be given free rein. Indeed, the kitchen can be home to a changing tableau of fresh foods, favorite postcards or snapshots, magazine clip-pings, and even the children's latest artwork. No single surface is sacrosanct; walls, ceiling beams, counters and, of course, the refrigerator door can all serve for display. Because of the potential chaos, the key to any display is clarity. Everything should have a place, a place that it can be taken from and returned to: decoration and display should never interfere with the proper function-ing of the kitchen.

A collection needn't be massive. To keep an assortment of pottery from disappearing in this rather large kitchen, perfectly proportioned shelves are fitted with lace liners that draw the eye immediately.

A commodious Victorian kitchen mixes exuberant tastes in kitchen collections. Maxfield Parrish prints, below, throng the walls from ceiling to wainscotting, blending with English willowware and nineteenth century food and tobacco tins.

*E*at-in kitchens have a practical informality and they encourage companionship for the cook. In smaller ones, a drop leaf table stores compactly when not in service. An unusual shape such as this triangular wicker table, above, is also a fine choice. In a pullman kitchen, right, a freestanding table fits in comfortably.

A vast kitchen can be intimidating or sometimes even too large to work efficiently. The kitchen at right was scaled down by adding a table and chairs. The old wood table brings a 'country character' to the sleek, new counters and appliances, and serves as a work surface. The log cabin walls of the kitchen below are a good background for leisurely dining. At left, blackberries and peaches pose in a dreamy, colorful still-life.

The Wood Stove

The American love affair with the hearth is so long-standing that in many people's minds it is equated with the most nostalgic notion of home. In the mid-nineteenth century the wood stove assumed the responsibility of hearth as a more efficient heating and cooking source. So that the stovepipe could make use of its chimney, the cast iron wood stove and coal stove were sometimes connected into the fireplace.

With the introduction of gas and electricity, however, both wood and coal stoves fell out of favor, replaced by the range. Then, in the 1960s and 1970s, energy resources were re-evaluated, and this, together with a yearning for symbols of a simpler era, launched the renaissance of the wood stove as an essential companion to authentic American furnishings. Many manufacturers today produce wood stoves based on old foundry models. A wood stove does not require the major installation a new fireplace does and some new models offer lighter-toned finishes and have smaller, more delicate shapes appropriate to other rooms besides the kitchen.

For those who don't care to cut and stack wood but love the look of an old stove, some versions are being converted to gas, at left, or to electricity. The miniature stove in the lower corner was a salesman's model.

A collection of cookie cutters is displayed on this handsome old stove, set in its own brick cubby.

The Pie Safe

Before refrigeration, and even before wire screens, the pie safe was the place where baked goods, fresh from the fire, could cool without being sampled by insects. In primitive versions, holes were bored randomly through the wooden front and sides to create an aerated cupboard. Of course, any intelligent fly could walk in too!

Once tin began to be manufactured in sheet form, panels could be cut to fit on three, and sometimes all four sides, and piercing the tin resulted in hooked or barbed holes that discouraged pests. Piercing followed myriad patterns, from simple geometric shapes to highly intricate designs; elaborate patterns with more holes allowed more air to circulate around the cooling food.

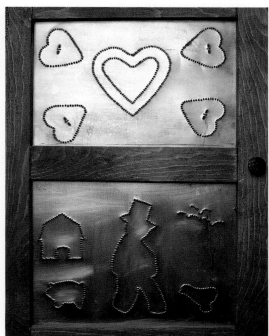

*P*ie safes today are collected to store almost anything, and they are pressed into service in every room in the house. One long-legged safe with an American motif, left, gathers a miscellany of treasures, including a berry basket and a Raggedy Ann. A new tin panel, above, reveals an infatuation with cookie-cutter motifs.

*W*hite elevates the beamed ceiling in a spacious kitchen, above. Delft tiles and a plastic laminate countertop introduce blue into the crisp scheme.

*T*he deep slate blue of the cabinetry, right, has the same color value as the plank floors. Mustard wainscoting warms a jazzy black and white kitchen, opposite.

The Colorful Kitchen

Because the kitchen is where the family spends most of its active time, color deserves some careful consideration. One approach is to add small doses of color in tandem with white or wood or stone, balancing it so the color adds energy and light to the room without becoming overbearing. Most food is warm in tone, so of all colors, blue, which appears in pure form in no food at all, is most complementary. That blue is a cool color actually enhances the appearance of food. Greens, reds, and other "food" colors should be chosen with care so that they do not set up a strident counterpoint to real food colors.

Wood tones, of course, harmonize with the color of grains and cereals. Accent colors on cookware, dinnerware, utensils, and linens that are displayed will refine the kitchen's tone. Food packages add their own graphic array of colors and shapes, and when organized on open shelves, will perk up a kitchen immeasurably. Antique tins, signs, children's artwork, and floorcloths all add color and vitality.

Trompe l'oeil is a time-honored paint technique for, literally, "fooling the eye." Historically it has been most effective in adding the illusion of space: to extend a hall through a make-believe doorway, for example, or to create an "outdoor" view through a painted door or window. The informality of the kitchen makes it ideal for whimsical treatments such as trompe l'oeil.

*P*ainted finishes around the kitchen artfully disguise less interesting materials. The ventilating hood, top right, is not wood, nor is the floor actually tile. New cabinets have been instantly aged with a hand-rubbed cloak of paint. A stippled wall, below right, mimics spatterware and brings color and texture to the kitchen. The painted door leads not to a barn, but to the garage, and cow never blinks, no matter what goes on in the kitchen.

Very few areas are gazed upon with more frequency than that in front of the sink. Here colorful doorstops have been recruited from floor duty.

Halls & Foyers

No matter how frequently we pass through a hall, we rarely pause to consider its decoration. Yet exactly because it is heavily trafficked and because, along with the entrance, it forms the first impression of the house, the hall deserves better treatment.

Generally the hall has a narrow shape, with plenty of wall space. This naturally converts into a gallery for photographs or flat art such as botanical prints or advertising art. The added height of the stair wall can be a dramatic setting for a large wall hanging, quilt, or painting. Strong overall lighting for the hall and stairs will promote enjoyment of the art as well as safety.

For reasons of space, hall furnishings are generally kept to a minimum, but can therefore be distinctive—a curious chair or a small table and coat rack may punctuate the area. A mirror will expand the space visually and reflect light. Beneath, a welcoming bowl of fresh flowers or potpourri can rest on a hall table, which is a logical place to leave mail and packages.

A tall reproduction pine settle draped with a vibrant quilt dominates this lantern-lit, stenciled hall, top left. Warm tones of thick adobe walls, stripped wood flooring, and "vigas" (lodgepole pine beams) are

illuminated by a skylight in a southwestern hall, top right. Tiered displays utilize the entire wall in this hall, right. A lantern, bonnets, and chairs hang from a pegboard; above, flowers hang to dry from a picture rail.

A second floor landing now displays a collection of antique coverlets on specially-designed racks. Air circulates easily around the coverlets to keep them free of moths.

*T*he stenciled entrance, left, is a generous arched space that admits visitors into the house in unhurried and uncramped fashion.

A gentle feline, above, purrs its greeting from a hooked rug in this sunlit entrance.

*T*his hand-tinted checkerboard floor links the foyer to an adjacent hall, right, where a table holds an eclectic arrangement of tree fungi and birds' nests.

Gameboards

Whether painted by professional sign painters or amateurs, old gameboards display a simple graphic inventiveness that has elevated them almost to the status of folk art. Adorned with imaginative decoration, most of these colorful boards date from the nineteenth century when game playing, especially with portable boards, was a common social pasttime. Checkerboards far outnumber other formats, although the games were many and varied and included such classics as Parcheesi, backgammon, darts, and Chinese checkers. Today, less well-known games such as Wheel of Fortune, Agon, and the Mill Game are most sought after by collectors.

*T*wo Parcheesi boards, one of linoleum inlay, top, and the other of stained wood, below, illustrate the graphic skills of early board makers.

*C*lustered together, gameboards animate a wall, far left. Agon, at top left, and a Mill Game, at center right, are rare boards. A checkers tournament, left, revives the beloved checkerboard.

Signs of wear enhance value.

Most gameboards were constructed of wood and then painted, but examples do exist of boards crafted in other materials, such as linoleum. The variations possible within the circumscribed format of games such as checkers or Parcheesi are profuse and sometimes surpris-ing. Parcheesi especially adapted brilliantly to stylization and variations on its format. Around the edges, some boards have separate compartments to hold playing pieces; these were often embellished with intricate figurative or abstract designs because they endured less abuse than the "playing field."

Stairways

In early American houses, staircases were strictly functional, and tended to be both extremely narrow and steep, sandwiched behind or scrolled around a massive center chimney. As houses grew in size, so did the space and prominence accorded to stairs. In center hall designs the staircase became the focal point of the entrance, with an appropriate increase in grace and dignity. Yet despite their improved status, staircases are still often considered only as a decorating afterthought.

This is really unfortunate, as stairs are well-suited for experimenting with various decorating ideas: they are generally smaller, more manageable areas that be-cause of their central position show off any attention accorded them. Paint techniques especially are effective on staircases, where their boldness or delicacy will be noticeable yet not overpowering as in a larger area. Walls alongside staircases can be covered with a surprising variety of objects—framed art, dried flowers, ceramic tiles, gameboards, a collection of babydoll quilts—which are then enjoyed each time the stairs are trod. Stair coverings should be durable, and stairs are excellent spots for rugs or runners too small for a full room, or which have deteriorated with age, leaving only strips of usable material.

A wall of photographs spans six generations of one family, left. A delightful mix of frames adds to the highly personal feeling of the display. Adult and child alike can "read" their way upstairs via these stenciled alphabet risers, right. Below left, wood baskets, buckets, and boxes sweep upwards beneath a delicately stenciled frieze. Stoneware jugs, below right, are displayed with framed antique samplers.

As places of transition, staircases allow more scope for decorative treatments such as stenciling, far left, or a simple paint finish, above , whose wear attests to the vitality of the house. Landings offer a sunny place for reading.

Country Bedrooms

E very other room in the house responds to a social function: cooking, dining, entertaining, or working. The bedroom, by contrast, answers intensely personal and private needs . . . the longing for solitude, for quiet after a strenuous day, and for retreat and rest. In a country-style home, the living, dining, and kitchen spaces are often linked, either by a consciously designed open plan or at least by open doors and passages. Bedrooms are separate from these spaces because the bedroom is an old-fashioned sanctuary, a refuge, a haven.

Just as the kitchen might be termed the energetic heart of the house, so the bedroom can be thought of as the still soul. The country bedroom is, first and foremost, a peaceful, calm place, whether decorated sparsely or in a more layered style, and its gentle colors and soft furnishings should foster a sense of repose.

The bed, of course, dominates, if only by its size, but it should not humble the space. In a sense, it is a world within a world: the fabrics and linens that clothe it are fine, soothing accents. Linens may be plain or adorned with lace or embroidery; the pillows may be simply encased or plumped in ruffled shams. Pretty wallpapers, paint embellished with sponging or striating, and paper borders all create an exquisite surround for the bed and its accessories. For privacy, windows can be veiled with translucent curtains that permit daylight to filter through. Photographs of family and friends and personal mementos add a mood of intimacy.

In the child's room and the guest room, the comfort of others is a paramount concern. The special touches — toys for children, flowers, books, and magazines for guests — warm these rooms with consideration so that they, too, become welcoming, cozy retreats.

Romantic Bedrooms

The romantic bedroom is a serene and gentle hideaway from the busyness of family life. Pale tranquil colors, diaphanous and fragile fabrics, and delicate textures characterize both the background and the accessories of a romantic bedroom. Pretty wallcoverings or paint applied in muted tones will instill a gentleness in the room. Romantic does not have to mean pink or feminine—merely warm and inviting—and light as much as anything else can determine its mood. Its strength should always be tempered and diffused, by gauzy curtains at the windows and by decorative lampshades, and by bouncing the main light off the walls or the ceiling.

The romantic bedroom typically lavishes its attention on a beautifully detailed bed that is in itself a sanctuary. Whether a four-poster or canopy bed, a wrought iron or a brass confection, the bed in a romantic setting is often veiled in hangings and linens. Lace-edged or complementary patterned sheets and drifts of soft pillows accentuate the lushness and comfort of the romantic bedroom.

*I*n two graceful rooms, left and below, canopies were hung directly from the ceiling, both to dramatize the link between the bed and the structure of the room, and to make the ceiling itself appear higher. Also, neither bed actually has posts, which this construction camouflaged.

*H*inting at romance both past and future, antique valentines collect under glass on a dressing table, left. A cherished photo is slipped in among the cards. Flowers are a romantic year-round reminder of springtime, both in color and tender fragrance, a private indulgence worth the cost.

*W*arm sunlight floods onto floral print pillows on this feminine bed finished with a double-layered skirt. A splashy paint finish on the stucco walls and white floors are rustic touches.

The Four-Poster Bed

Four-poster beds were originally designed with heavy drapes on all sides to protect their occupants from drafts and cold at night. Many early versions elevated the bed high above the floor, so high in fact that steps were needed. But while the posts of the bed defined its structure, they also conferred the stature of a revered object, since four-posters had aristocratic connections and were expensive to construct. When dressed in fine linens, quilts, and shams, the bed often became a conscious symbol of luxury and wealth.

Today, of course, we choose four-posters not for their insulating qualities but rather for their inherent romance and style. Liberated from their original function, the designs have now become far more varied. Four-posters range from robust, overtly masculine beds with heavy head and foot posts to slender feminine designs such as the pencil post bed. Some four-posters have canopies and a few are adorned with curtains, but all capture the romance that is part of the timeless appeal of this bed.

Daubed in blue milk paint, above, this cannonball four-poster has a simple pediment-shaped backboard. A tapered pencil post bed, left, was stained black and now shines, pure and simple, against a bold checkerboard floor. Plain flannel sheets on the bed ward off chills; the Hudson Bay blanket is a reminder of northern climes.

*T*he serpentine canopy on a new four-poster, right, will lift off to attach netting or hangings. A home-spun blanket is draped over a rustic quilt rack next to the bed. The rugged outline of the heart-shaped back of this pine four-poster, below, em-phasizes its silhouette. Its blankets are punctuated by chenille striations and stars.

Machine-crocheted netting drifts over a gently curved canopy, top left, and filters light from the nearby window. Floral bed coverings and pale pine furniture enhance the summery feeling. Lengths of plain, unbleached muslin, below, were pinned to a canopy frame. Such a modern interpretation of the traditional canopy costs little and is easily installed on a full-frame four-poster. Sheets, shirred and gathered on thin rods attached to the ceiling, right, form an elegant canopy.

Bed Hangings

I n medieval times—and during America's own colonial days—bed hangings created islands of warmth and privacy within otherwise drafty, and often public, rooms. Today, doors ensure privacy and radiators warmth, so bedhangings function more as visual enrichments for beds. When a bed is hugely proportioned, a canopy and curtains soften the overall effect, and in concert with a dust ruffle, pillow shams, and fluffy bedcoverings, diffuse attention from the frame. In a chilly room, of course, pulling bedcurtains will thwart the cold, a bonus when the thermostat is turned low as an economical and energy-efficient measure in winter.

Canopies are quintessentially romantic, and languorously draped hangings ease the harsh lines of modern house and apartment bedrooms. While the most popular canopy is full-length, half-testers—those that extended a fraction of the bed's length—are still common, especially in the South. Equally, the drapery can function as a headboard, or double thicknesses of sheets can be hung to form the canopy and curtains. Such sheet hangings can easily be put into the washer for cleaning or changed to match a new color scheme.

The Colorful Bedroom

Because the bedroom should be an oasis of calm within the normal activity of the house, subdued colors, natural tones, and gentle textures work best to relax the environment. These colors and tones are also the friendliest and tend to be the most becoming. Bold, bright colors can be too stimulating; they might overpower a bedroom. Deep or intense shades are more restful and do look lush, but when selected for the country bedroom they should be muffled with gentle lighting. Dark colors can be tamed with a tiny print or relieved with a lighter stripe; intense colors, by neutral trim.

Bright colors as accents are energizing, and the visual punch of a graphic quilt or the splash of a full-blown bouquet of wildflowers will enliven the country bedroom. The classic all-white scheme can be at its best in a bedroom. Here the textures—of lace, percale, and cutwork linen—add dramatic impact, and accessories assume a greater importance against this neutral background. Soft, hushed pastels such as peach, rose, seafoam green, and jade flatter both a bedroom and its occupants. This is why so many bedlinens, wallcoverings, draperies, and rugs come in those colors.

The lighting of the room is the key to the success of any color. In contrast with a room that receives only thin northern light, an east-facing bedroom warmed each morning with sunlight will more easily tolerate paler and cooler greens or blues for the dominant scheme. In mood, the softer, low-key light of table lamps creates a more intimate atmosphere with any color scheme and is more versatile than the even, overhead illumination of a central ceiling fixture.

Color in the bedroom usually takes its cue from the background, but a special object such as a painting, a wall-mounted quilt, or an antique rug may also inspire the design. Again, neither the color nor the object itself should be too imposing; both should work almost subliminally to create and enhance a comforting sense of repose and retreat.

In a bedroom under the eaves, left, foggy-toned linens set the mood, along with a gray-green wall in the colors of a night sea. Curtainless windows let the sun flood in, highlighting the lacy top sheet and rich tones of the antique rope bed.

Yards and yards of ruffled white eyelet play off the richness of a brick wall, giving this bedroom, below, a light, airy feeling.

Decorating with Quilts

No single item more epitomizes country than the quilt. Humble in origin, practical in intent, it is a glorious reminder of craftsmanship, and of an unschooled talent and timeless eye for beauty. The earliest quilts were simple: two pieces of cloth sandwiched a core of wool or cotton batting, and the layers were joined together by running stitches. But quilt design soon grew in complexity and became a creative outlet for women seeking respite from the arduous rituals of everyday life.

Culling scraps of fabrics, mainly from worn clothing, quiltmakers cut basic geometric shapes—squares, circles, triangles—which they combined in imaginative patterns. These were then pieced together in blocks. Once the blocks were sewn together to form the quilt top, women of the community would gather to complete the quilt, stitching the layers over a frame. These festive "quilting bees" were rich in shared stories and gossip.

The names bestowed on the quilts reflect the women's observations and concerns: "Tree of Life," "Rob Peter to Pay Paul," and hundreds of other names attest to the imaginative interpretations of their world.

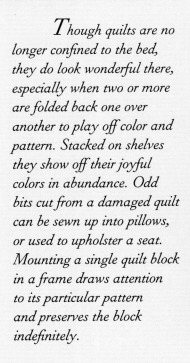

*T*hough quilts are no longer confined to the bed, they do look wonderful there, especially when two or more are folded back one over another to play off color and pattern. Stacked on shelves they show off their joyful colors in abundance. Odd bits cut from a damaged quilt can be sewn up into pillows, or used to upholster a seat. Mounting a single quilt block in a frame draws attention to its particular pattern and preserves the block indefinitely.

These blocks of Amish quilts demonstrate the depth and intensity of Amish design.

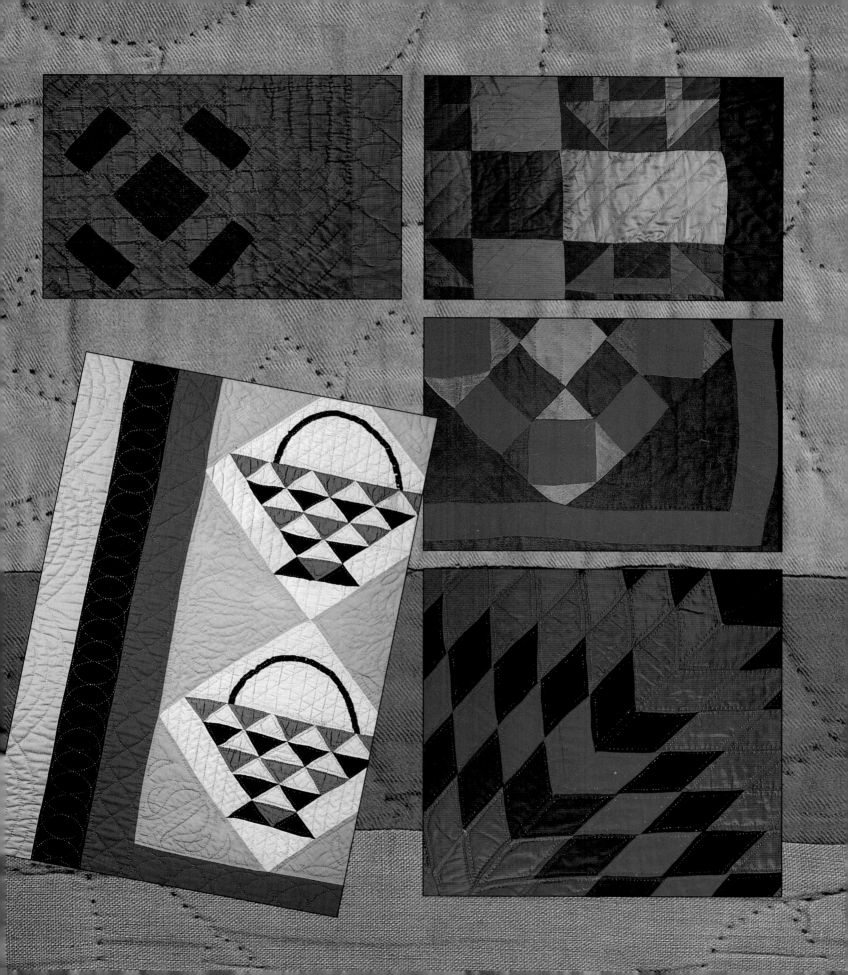

Airing quilts outdoors refreshes them and prevents them from becoming musty. Too much sun, however, will fade their colors. Quilts in direct sunlight should be turned periodically to protect their brilliancy.

Bed-Living Rooms

A live-in bedroom captures the nostalgic best of the keeping room—to relax, sleep, and eat in one place—and simultaneously retains its essential allure, that of a private cocoon. During the day, the bedroom is often one of the quietest and most secluded rooms in the house. A writing desk or hobby table, a window seat, an easy chair, a chaise, or a settee, a dining table: any or all of these, given the space, will transform the room into a self-contained world to be enjoyed at any time of day, away from cares and daily routine.

Generally, the furnishings of a live-in bedroom are smaller in scale and informal in mood—a comfortable loveseat or two-cushion sofa scattered with plenty of cushions, for example. Generous storage space keeps clothes and linens tucked from sight, to enhance a feeling of ordered serenity. A moveable screen hides a writing table or the bed, as appropriate, and brings a quick change of mood to the room.

Lighting should be as versatile as the furniture since it may have to be both functional—over a work area—and atmospheric—next to the bed. A combination of floor and table lamps permits the mood of the lighting to be carefully controlled. Putting the main lighting on a dimmer switch allows continuously varied effects.

A night table, far left, that converts into a writing desk and bookcases that serve as storage for bedside items, below left, add comfort to bedrooms. Plump wing chairs, near left, pulled up to a window are inviting seating for a bedroom and a separate table for breakfast or late-night supper is a particularly congenial addition. Plenty of reading matter and a comfortable sofa beneath a window make this bedroom, below, a welcoming retreat.

The embroidered linens known by the colloquialism "turkeywork" were made in great quantities during the Victorian era. Following favorite patterns in books or periodicals, women traced their chosen designs onto linen. Then, working with colorfast thread, usually a clear red or more rarely a blue, they sewed along the outlines in a simple backstitch.

Guest Rooms

Whether for a night, a weekend, or longer, a guest becomes a genuine member of the family. As a comfortable place for rest and privacy, the room reserved for guests should tangibly extend a welcome and act as a visible token of the host's affection and respect. If the guest room is not a multipurpose space, a den or living room for example, it is probably occupied far less often than other rooms in the house. It takes a special effort to prevent it from acquiring the coldness of an unlived-in room, or becoming a warehouse for left-over bits and pieces of furniture.

Because it is frequently a "spare" room, a guest room can be used as something of a lab for decorating ideas that might ultimately translate into other rooms in the home. Experimenting in this setting is fun—and liberating. An intriguing paint technique or a lovely but novel wallcovering might be tried out in the guest room first. Antiques obviously endure less abuse in this room, so fine or fragile pieces can be placed here without concern. Whimsical or humorous accents, too, work well in a guest room; it is a great gift to bring a smile to a visitor. A vase of fresh cut flowers, specially chosen reading material, a good reading light, warm blankets, and a comfortable seat make a guest feel at home.

Here is a guest room that plays two roles. With a flick of its cover, the dressing table converts into a sewing station, and the guest room into a crafts center. In fact, all the fabrications for this provincial-style room were run up right on the spot. Cabinets that are faced with salvaged windows store fabrics, patterns, and sewing supplies. Threads are stashed in an antique spool cabinet which doubles as a bedside table.

*P*lain or pretty, spartan or lavishly appointed, a guest room is home away from home for a friend or relative, and so must be as thoughtful and welcoming as possible. Best-quality mattresses and pillows indicate a caring touch, as do crisp linens and beautiful bedcovers, top left. A room as spare as the blue one, top, compliments guests by offering them cherished antiques and accessories.

A softly decorated room, by contrast, bottom, mixes new and old with an artful hand. Here the owner experimented with an unlikely color combination—warm eggshell and cool green—which worked because both tones have a similar color value. These rooms meet a guest's needs, providing comfort, light, and quiet. Sensuous accents such as flowers, scent, and extra pillows are considerate touches that make a difference.

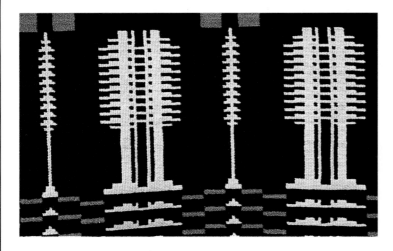

*L*ightweight overshot and heavier jacquard coverlets are still used primarily on the bed; remnants make up into tidy pillow covers.

*E*ven a tiny block of coverlet is too good to waste, and can be mounted and framed for display.

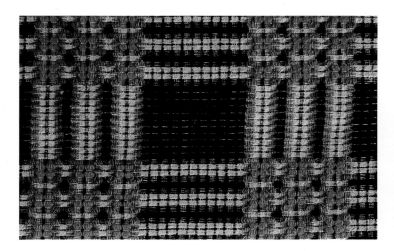

Coverlets

Coverlets, handwoven and later machine crafted, were made by the thousands during the first half of the nineteenth century. Uniquely American, they originated in the East, though many of the coverlets being collected today come from the Midwest. Hand-loomed "overshot" coverlets have soft, heavy weft threads drawn through a lighter background in various geometric patterns. Women bestowed names on their designs that reflected their personal concerns, be they religious, ethnic, natural, or political. Eventually, professional weavers and itinerant craftsmen, all male, made coverlets on heavier looms they carried with them. After 1820, many weavers added a punch-card control feature called the Jacquard which enabled them to develop designs of astonishing complexity and naturalism.

Both types of coverlet are reversible; the preferred dyes for the warp were indigo blue and madder red, although brown and tan were also known. Very few jacquards combined two or more warp colors and collectors look for finishing touches such as fringe and elaborate borders, which add to the value of a coverlet.

Weavers of jacquards often signed, dated, and signified place of manufacture, as well as the name of the buyer. After the Civil War, when inexpensive factory-woven fabrics became commonplace, coverlets virtually disappeared. Overshots, however, are being produced again today.

Reversible coverlets can be flipped according to the season, showing a pale side for summer and darker for winter. Combining coverlets, whether overshot or jacquard, will play up their strong graphic qualities and rich textures.

The high contrast corrugations of a log-and-chink wall are a perfect foil for the geometric quilts and coverlet. The nineteenth century Ohio-made coverlet, right, exhibits a bold, abstract design.

Children's Rooms

Children's rooms are castles and caves and magic kingdoms. A kid's room is a stronghold against scary monsters and in the next instant, a portal to paradise. Here, surrounded by their toys, dolls, and animals—by the things they love, scaled to their size— children expand upon their fantasies and, in so doing, enrich their lives.

Historically, the child's room is relatively new. In Colonial America, children played and slept in the same room as their parents, and their toys were simple found objects intended to educate them in grown-up rituals. Nowadays, a child's room is often a frenzy of toys, books, and mechanical equipment.

The country bedroom, by contrast, tries to balance imagination with privacy and restraint. Cozy, secure, and safe, it intimates that play comforts as well as educates. Materials such as natural wool and rag rugs require little upkeep and can endure the assaults of years of enthusiastic games. Children's quilts are both warm and whimsical, and toys are stored in an old-fashioned toy chest. As children grow older, the quiet comforts of a country bedroom mature easily and gracefully with them. Country children's rooms are magical at heart, and as Goldilocks would say, they feel "just right."

Chunky hand-hewn logs brace a pair of bunk beds wedged between window and wall, establishing two protected islands for imaginary games, right.

A brass bed and pretty linens create a fantasy room for dreaming, day or night, for an older girl. Treasured clothing such as christening dresses and caps and vintage lacy dresses and camisoles have an air of languid romance.

Children often enjoy sleeping in a grown-up bed like this brass relic, right. Plenty of dolls and bears make the room cozier. An embroidered tea towel and a turkeywork duster float in the window. Repeating goose borders, below, at both ceiling and baseboard bring a child's room down to scale. The trundle bed pulls out for sleepovers or as a comfortable place for games.

Because a child's room is also a haven, nesting the bed against a wall provides a protected circle for slumbering, above.

Peter Rabbit and his brothers and sisters are playful touches on this diminutive tea set.

Dolls & Toys

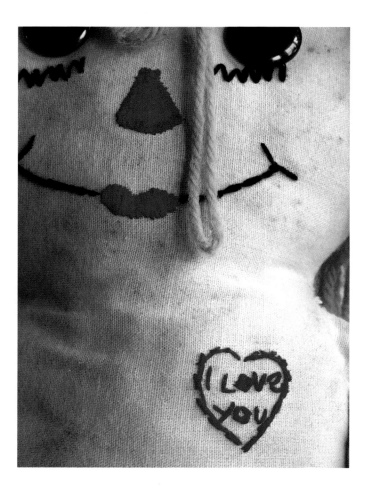

Raggedy Anns and Andys express true affection for their owners with embroidered hearts that pledge "I Love You," right.

Raggedy Ann was born in 1918 for the sick daughter of Johnny Gruelle, who renewed an old doll to entertain her.

During the Colonial era, children were expected to contribute to the family chores and given virtually no time for play. The Puritan ethic, furthermore, considered play and toys frivolous. By the mid-eighteenth century though, many children, at least in more affluent families, began to be treated as children and not merely miniature adults. Toys were made specifically for them, though many were expected to educate, not simply to amuse. Blocks with letters on them, for example, acquainted a child with the alphabet. Tops, kites, hoops, and dolls were purely pleasurable.

Primitive homemade dolls were sewn from rag scraps, devised from dried corn cobs and husks, or made of wood. Exceptional dolls might have bisque or porcelain faces and hands. These early dolls, too, could be imbued with meaning. Amish dolls do not have faces, for example, as the Amish feel it is heretic to behold the image of self or person. During the nineteenth century, in response to the Victorian adoration of childhood, dolls and toys of all kinds, from rocking horses to mechanical games, were mass-produced. By the 1870s almost two hundred toy manufacturers were in operation across the United States. In 1892, another mass-produced favorite made its appearance: the toy soldier. Today both old and new dolls and bears, soldiers and bunnies still hold children, and many adults, in thrall.

*Keeping each other
company, two rag dolls sit
on a woven seat chair.*

A well-loved bunny
gazes over events from his
comfortable perch.

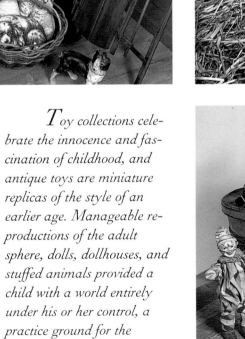

*T*oy collections cele-
brate the innocence and fas-
cination of childhood, and
antique toys are miniature
replicas of the style of an
earlier age. Manageable reproductions of the adult
sphere, dolls, dollhouses, and
stuffed animals provided a
child with a world entirely
under his or her control, a
practice ground for the
business of growing up.

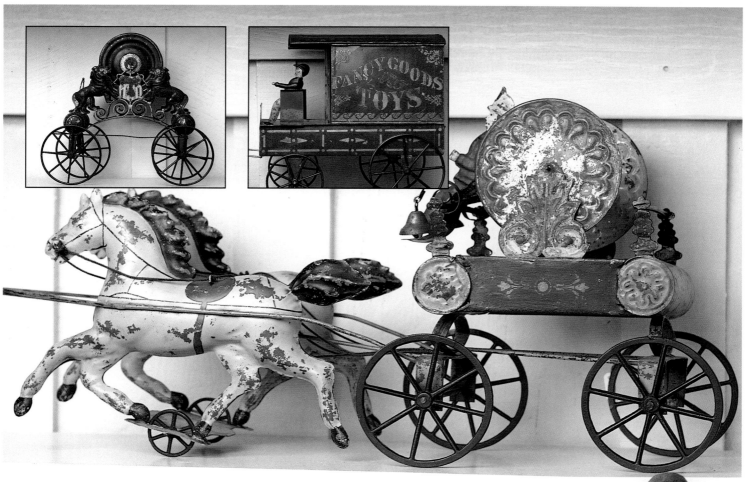

*M*otion — *the faster the better* — *thrills children, and these wheeled toys, careening around a nursery or hallway, probably accompanied a toddler's headlong rush at independence.*

Minutely detailed, they hinted at a great world outside a childish ken, and now remind us of an era long past yet fondly remembered.

Teddy Bears

Who can resist a teddy bear? Baptized "Teddy" for President Theodore Roosevelt, who turned his gun away from a stray bear cub during a hunt, the chummy bruin has amused Americans since 1902. Now our most beloved stuffed toy, Teddy's soulful shoe button eyes, wistful embroidered smile, and upturned nose endear him to us; his chubby arms reach out for a hug. So enamored of Teddy are we that children often find their favorites usurped by adults, who regard them with rare reverence.

Bears are christened not only Teddy and Theodore and Edward, but Aloysius, Amanda, William, and Bernard. Endowed with personal biographies, bears assume idiosyncratic dress and habits. Some are natty, social, and self-assured; others are slightly demure and retiring; some are eccentric and some almost stylishly down-at-heel. Many attend tea parties while others frequent only football games. Today, Teddies are our most sought-after toy. Just a decade ago, a balding, tattered Teddy might fetch a hundred dollars or so at auction; today Teddies of certain lineage—a Steiff, Shackman, or Ideal bear, for example—have increased in value ten-fold.

*T*eddy bears that predate World War II, left, are valuable antiques. The oldest bears, and the most highly regarded by collectors, have elongated muzzles, humpbacks, moveable arms and legs, and are stuffed with excelsior, a strawlike material, right. Some bears have plush fur pelts, rarest in angora, while others do with plain wool. Steiff bears, imported from Germany and still manufactured today, above, must wear their distinctive ear buttons and yellow and red tags to retain full value.

A miniature cotton cloth bear casts a benign gaze over the world from his perch in a candle box.

The solitary bear is proud and independent, but may appear lonely, too. Better to bunch bears, as at right, in a companionable arrangement. A wagon, a settee, even a shelf will serve — any useful place to put things in. Bears also enjoy gathering under the Christmas tree, as it reminds them of their birth as gifts.

*T*he more affection and handling enjoyed by a much-loved bear, the more dear it is to the ardent collector. Bald patches and missing tufts in a bear's coat only testify to his happy life, and replacement parts may diminish the value of a bear. A substitute limb should match its mate in texture and hue; new eyes should be made of authentic material such as black glass. Stuffy, above, is in a party mood in a 1933 paper hat; he attended a Teddy Bear Rally in New England.

The Outdoors

Americans love the outdoors and always have. Even when pioneers pushed the limits of the frontier, taming woods, plains, and wilderness into farms and later towns, cities, and suburbs, they never lost sight of the land. The love of land persists, and is visible even in the centers of our most crowded cities, in small yards and tiny gardens, and empty lots bursting with plucky flowers and produce.

The American dream endures: a house with a porch, a garden, and a backyard. A naturally sociable place, part extension of the house, and part extension of the yard, the porch evolved from a small portico sheltering the front door into a full-scale outdoor room with open, screened, or glassed-in walls. Some porches cover the entire facade of a house; others tuck into the elbow at the join of the body and wing of the home. Beyond the welcoming shade of the porch, the garden and yard are framed by fences, accented by outbuildings, pools, and furniture, extending the comforts of indoors into the freshness of out.

Considerations of scale, color, and texture count as much in outdoor living spaces as they do inside, and when the porch, garden, and yard are well-designed, they complement the house, bringing indoors and out into harmony. Generally, country gardens and yards tend to be informal. Flowers, shrubs, and trees are not confined to formal beds but mass and spill over with all the rambling and colorful charm of an English cottage garden. Hammocks, wicker or twig chairs, certainly a picnic table and chairs, and other comfortable, unpretentious furnishings suit this relaxed mood.

The garden and yard nourish the house they surround both spiritually and tangibly; flowers, herbs, and vegetables from the garden enhance table and decor, and prove that country decorating is more than an amalgam of paint, paper, fabric, and collectibles. Country decorating embraces living elements as well.

Open Porches

Irst contrived as shelter for the entrance to the house, the porch has evolved into a more significant "room" that naturally links house and yard, indoors and out. From the mid-nineteenth century onward, porches—large or small, elaborate or simple—were mandatory features of virtually every new home.

In its most utilitarian guise, the open porch is a carefree work room or outdoor studio. A logical intermediary between garden and kitchen, it can handle simple garden tasks. Impervious to soil and water, the porch is a cool refuge for sorting vegetables, potting plants, and arranging fresh cut flowers. A breezy alternative to

the steamy summer kitchen, here cooking and kitchen chores seem less arduous.

Weatherproof and weatherworn furniture suit the porch best: wood, wicker, and wrought iron are not just the most popular materials, but also in keeping with the mood of most porches.

As well as a place the family naturally gravitates to in hot weather, the porch extends the first sign of welcome to visitors, and so should be inviting. Evergreen plants or dried flower and herb wreaths decorate the area year-round in even the harshest climates, while masses of fresh cut flowers are lovely in warmer weather.

*T*he porch extension
to a log cabin, left, converts
to a potting shed and harvest
center during the growing
season. Cottage Windsor
chairs, field baskets, and drying wildflowers and herbs all
hang out of reach until needed.
Painted wicker furniture
offers comfortable seating.

*O*n a grapevine-
shaded porch, right, dime-
store Windsor chairs were
renewed with the same blue
exterior paint used on the
clapboard house. For the
floor, bricks were laid on their
sides, without mortar, so dirt
can simply sift into the cracks.
A retired cupboard is a catch-
all for flowers, hats, and
newspapers, above.

Enclosed Porches

Once enclosed, the porch becomes a sheltered outdoor room for socializing and entertaining, retaining all the light and airy charm of an open porch yet offering protection from insects and inclement weather. One of the delights of glass and screen, or a combination of the two, is that they enclose a porch without visually confining it.

When screened, the porch becomes a far more versatile part of the home. Not only can it serve as an outdoor living or dining room, but it can also double as a cool refuge for sleeping when the temperature soars. Here, a beautiful view or the colors and textures of a well-placed flower bed or trees can be enjoyed. During cold weather, fragile potted plants can be wintered over, safe from damaging sub-zero temperatures; and year-round, exotics such as cacti and succulents, fuschias, orchids, camellias, and begonias will flourish in the windows of a glass-enclosed porch.

*W*icker thrives on the porch, left, because it breathes in the heat and humidity. A trio of wicker rockers and a southern "plantation" cane chair provide plenty of seating. Flagstones are cool and durable underfoot in a screened porch, above. A wrought iron daybed invites post-tea relaxation.

*M*ulti-paned windows set in ribbon formation create walls of glass for a spacious porch, far left. A glazed ceiling has turned this porch into a full sunroom.

A Summer Screened House

*S*creened houses and gazebos are the simplest of constructions; mere wisps of trellis and screen mesh to attract the lightest breeze on sultry summer days. At the end of a pier, this airy screened house perches on pilings above a pond, offering respite from the broiling sun and buzzing mosquitoes. Decorated with white wicker furnishings, linens, and baskets, the house is cooled and kept dry by canvas shades which unfurl on all sides from behind scalloped cornices. Guests can stay overnight in the iron bed or on a Texas daybed, both plumped with unexpectedly elegant embroidered pillows, as well as easy care bedding. Meals are rolled down to the screened house on a wicker tea cart, which stands in as an end table or buffet when locked into place next to the dining table.

Garden Rooms

Conservatories, which became so popular in Victorian times, are sunlit spaces that are almost like outdoor rooms. More suitable for living than their strictly practical cousin, the humid working greenhouse, they can be one of the most economical home additions because most models are pre-fabricated and attach to the house. Conservatories are fanciful places filled with wrought iron or wicker furniture, exotic plants, and even birds. Ideally, they should have good ventilation and insulation to keep them cool even in the height of summer and cozy on the coldest winter day.

Like so many garden structures—conservatories, summer houses, and shady leaf-entwined arbors—gazebos have a wonderfully romantic aura. Here is a place, shaded from the sun, to read, or to entertain or, as its name suggests, simply to relax and enjoy the view.

A log grape arbor, above, gives dappled shade from the sun to the seating area beneath.

The gazebo and the greenhouse are two very different outdoor rooms: one presents cool shade, the other warm sunlight. Built from logs and lattice, the rustic gazebo, near left, was set under a tree to ensure total shade. Twig chairs are easily carried into the gazebo for larger gatherings. The sunny conservatory, far left, is a perfect setting for dining. To counteract the heat, shades can be drawn over the tempered glass, but in cool months sun streaming in provides welcome warmth.

Garden Furnishings

As much as flowerbeds, ribbons of hedge, stands of trees, or other natural elements, planters, sculpture, and decorative objects add personality and visual interest to gardens and yards. Like furniture, they are often placed close to the house, to visually extend and blend the boundary of indoors and out. But a picnic table set under a leafy tree, or a garden bench poised before a beautiful view, or a sundial or any kind of weathered found object will add a sense of surprise and intrigue to an obscure corner of the garden.

A birdhouse can perch on stilts, top left, hang on hooks, or nail directly to a tree, and their visitors add sight and sound to the garden. Fences "make good neighbors" and form picturesque garden boundaries, left.

Sealed to withstand weather, favorite antique barnyard creatures, like the geese "flatties," right, stride over the grass.

Wicker is a natural choice for summer gardens, left. During warm weather, seating areas around the house and garden only heighten the appeal of the outdoors. A heart-shaped basket, above, filled with fresh-cut garden flowers, testifies to a sentimental yearning for perpetual spring.

Gardens

An old wagon spends its retirement hosting a cluster of white geraniums.

Garden design begins with a simple but ever-changing palette of leaf and grass greens, earth browns, and sky blues. The variety and success of the colors and textures imposed on this basic scheme speak ardently of a gardener's skill and individuality. Some gardens delight in a riot of color, while others are meant to seduce in a single shade, such as the all-white garden.

Decorating with plants is an endeavor akin to decorating with fabric: not only color, but texture and sheen matter tremendously. The balance of tall versus short, ruffly versus prickly foliage, and small versus large blooms is important. An experienced gardener considers the blooming order to manage the entire effect. But whether formal or exuberant, tousled or tidy, a country garden is truly a constant delight.

This rustic open porch, above, is a shady spot for everyone when the sun gets too hot.

A fence border, right, or an arched gate, top left, define the boundaries of a home garden. Fences, gates, and trellises are also good grooming aids, training trailing vines and blooms.

A Summer Playhouse

Perhaps what lies at the heart of the American love of outdoor "rooms"—porches, gazebos, and the like—is the memory of that original sylvan fantasy, the treehouse. Children as much as adults want a place all their own, and one that combines privacy with a sense of adventure is all the more satisfying.

This secluded refuge was built among the branches of a venerable live oak, which offers both a strong foundation and a natural fence. Salvaged wood was cheap and lends the perfect rustic feeling, so the messiest games are appropriate in this rugged house.

While a mascot guards the fort, the adventurer can scan the field from the branches of his treetop aerie.

A humanitarian deer trophy, pieced together from scraps of wood, watches over the wilderness retreat.

Stocked with binoculars and bird food, arrowheads, maps, books, and butterfly specimens, the treehouse serves as home base for a young naturalist. A bandana-print sleeping bag is a toasty place to camp out.

Creating the
COUNTRY
Look

Country Crafts

One of the primary pleasures of country decorating is its accessibility. A country house, even when filled with antique treasures, is a livable, inviting place, and country collectibles are desirable in great measure because they've been handled and used and loved for years. The creators of such handmade necessities as quilts, baskets, hooked rugs, and so on, took the time and thought to imbue their work with simple beauty. It is this personal stamp that embodies the best of Country.

Made at home and used at home, crafts have always been an integral part of country living. So what better and more satisfying way to express one's pleasure in and devotion to a home than by making a highly individual rug or quilt.

Our rule of thumb in choosing the crafts for this section was the same as that used for choosing items for a home: respond first and foremost to delight and imagination. Some of the projects that follow are intended more as suggestions or inspirations. The great beauty of these timeless crafts is that, once mastered, they can be adapted and modified to your own patterns or ideas almost endlessly. Some of the following crafts are cornerstones of country decorating, like paint techniques and quilt making; some are inherently charming, like handmade wreaths and potpourris; others are for arts recently revived, like candlewicking.

The difficulty and time involved also span a wide range. Ice candles or potpourris can be completed by the novice in a few hours or an afternoon; the quilts and rugs require a certain basic skill and, of course, a greater investment of time. All of the crafts will provide pleasure, enhance any home, and create something that can be handed down to generations to come.

The Schoolhouse:
A Symbol of Country

The labels on home-made preserves each display a different country motif. The schoolhouse quilt at right forms a background to a collection of handcarved wooden pigs. It was too narrow to fit most beds, so the owner was able to buy it for very little.

The hooked rug, above, is ideal for a child's room. At right, a Schoolhouse quilt block provides a striking focus for this craft-filled living room.

*T*he Schoolhouse is
*a perennial motif in country
decorating, epitomizing its
spirit and symbolizing the
virtues of home and community. Though its exact prove-
nance is unclear, the
schoolhouse motif is clearly
an American creation, taken
directly from the craftsper-
son's immediate world.
      Whether on a full-size
or crib quilt, hooked in a rug,
cross-stitched on a pillow, or
even stenciled on a floor,
wall, or label for homemade
preserves, the Schoolhouse
retains a lasting appeal.*

The Schoolhouse Quilt

The schoolhouse quilt on the bed, above, is a hand-made, modern rendition of the traditional design. By using only bright white and clear red, the bold graphics of the motif are enhanced and made to seem contemporary even in this era of modern schools.

INSTRUCTIONS

The finished quilt is approximately 63 inches square.

Materials: Rug wool, 57 inches wide, in Red No. 7250, 2 yards, and natural No. 100, 4½ yards, or any comparable colors (available from Dorr Mill Store, see p. 251); cotton or cotton-and-polyester thread in red and natural; lightweight cardboard or a manila folder; sharp pencil. Also (optional), a straightedge; a single-edge razor; red yarn for tufting.

To make the template, enlarge the schoolhouse pattern in the Diagram and transfer it to the manila folder or a piece of lightweight cardboard. Then cut out the four templates that form the schoolhouse.

On the wrong side of the red wool fabric, using the templates, trace and cut out sixteen of each element that makes up the schoolhouse. Use a single-edge blade and metal straightedge to ensure clean cutting.

From the natural wool tear sixteen 12½-inch squares. Be sure to tear carefully and slowly; the torn edge adds to the primitive look of the finished quilt.

Stitch each square as follows. Arrange the red sections on a natural square to form the house and baste in place. Applique the sections to the square using red thread and a large machine zigzag stitch, stitching around the windows too. (Practice on scraps to get the proper stitch size.) Stitch all sixteen squares in this manner.

From the natural wool tear a 2¾-inches-wide strip and cut into twelve pieces, each 12½ inches long. Tear three more strips of a 2¾-by-56 inches. Make a section from the house squares and strips as follows. Join four squares with three of the 12½ inch strips. Baste two squares to the long edges of a strip, leaving 2 inches between squares. Zigzag stitch the squares to the strip and repeat to make a section with four squares long. Make three more sections in this manner.

Now join the four sections together using the 56-inch long strips and the zigzag stitch. If desired, you can join the sections so that the houses on two of them

face in the opposite direction from the other two as shown in the photograph, or place the sections so all the houses face in the same direction.

From the red wool, tear enough 1½-inch-wide strips to make four strips 59-inches long. Zigzag a strip to one edge of the quilt top, lapping the top over the strip by ¼-inch. Stitch the rest of the strips to the other edges in the same manner.

From the natural wool, tear 2-inch-wide strips to make four strips 62 inches long. Zigzag the strips to the edges of the quilt top as described for the red strips.

From the natural wool, tear and piece a backing to equal the size of the quilt top. Working on a large flat surface, place the top on the backing, with the wrong sides facing each other. Pin them together. If you desire, to secure the top to the backing you can zigzag stitch two or three rows across the quilt, stitching from the top over previously stitched lines. Or, secure the two layers together with tufting using red yarn.

Bind the quilt edges with the strips of red wool as follows. Tear enough of the 2-inch-wide strips to go around the edge. Turn up one on each strip ¾ inch and press. Join the strip to the edge by lapping ⅝ inch of the strip from the back of the quilt over the quilt edge, then pin and zigzag stitch. Turn 1¼- inch of the strip to the quilt front and zigzag stitch. Repeat this procedure for the other edges.

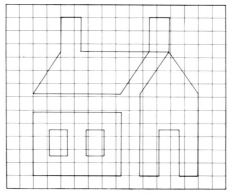

SCALE: 1 SQUARE = 1 INCH

The gently faded pinks in the basket quilt below cast a delicate rosy glow on the white bedroom. Remnants of old quilts make up the pillows at left, one in a calico print and another in a rare combination of floral and batik cottons.

The Basket Quilt

The basket motif is a perennial favorite for quilts. Evocative of the overflowing garden baskets of spring and summer, the basket is a symbol that is seen over and over again in traditional American homes, on wall stencils, on painted furniture, and most popularly, worked into fabric treatments such as the basket quilt. In a basket design, the geometric forms are arranged in a way that gives an impression of round softness.

Basket and other geometric quilt patterns can be fashioned on a sewing machine, above.

The Basket Quilt

INSTRUCTIONS

This Basket Quilt can be made by hand or on a machine and is large enough for a double bed. While it is not a terribly complicated pattern, you will need some sewing and piecing knowledge to complete it. But your efforts will be rewarded with a beautiful heirloom.

The finished quilt is approximately 70-by-82 inches. Press the fabric thoroughly before measuring and cut all pieces on the lengthwise or crosswise grain. Pieces must be cut exactly to the pattern if the quilt is to fit together properly.

Materials: 44-inch-wide cotton or cotton blend fabrics: 6⅝ yards White Calico; 1¾ yards Pink or other color; fabric for each block, 9-by-12 inches of Light Print fabric (A), 9-by-13 inches Dark Print (B); 81-by-

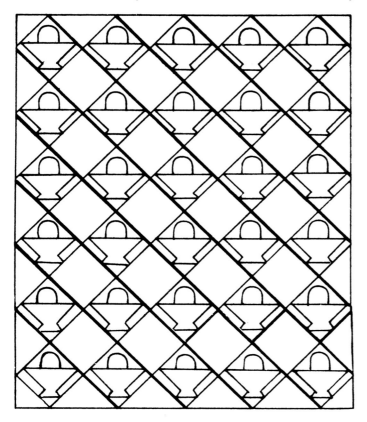

DIAGRAM A

96 inches Mountain Mist polyester quilt batt; sewing thread; quilting thread.

To cut: From White, cut a center back panel 44-by-83 inches, two side panels 14⅛-by-83 inches. Cut two side border strips 4¾-by-75 inches; top and bottom borders 4¾-by-70¾ inches. Cut twenty 9½-inch blocks. Cut nine 10-inch squares; cut diagonally to form eighteen half blocks. Cut two 7½-inch squares; then cut diagonally to form four quarter blocks. From Pink, cut fifteen 8¼-inch squares; cut diagonally to form thirty triangles. Cut fifteen 4¾-inch squares; cut diagonally to form thirty triangles. Cut sixty strips 2½-by-6 inches. Enlarge the quilt block. Trace the handle and add ¼-inch seam allowance around. For each block: from B, cut handle. Cut three 3-inch squares; cut diagonally to form six triangles (one extra). Cut one 2½-inch square. From A, cut six 3-inch squares; cut diagonally to form twelve triangles (one extra).

To make blocks (make thirty): (Use ⅜-inch seams.) Using the quilt block as a guide, piece blocks as follows: Sew an A and B triangle together along the diagonal to make a square. Make four more squares. Keeping A triangles at lower right, stitch a pieced square to the left-hand side of solid B square. Sew the second pieced square to the left-hand edge of resulting strip; sew A triangle to the left-hand end. Sew two pieced squares together; sew an A triangle to the left-hand end. Sew an A triangle to the left-hand side of the remaining square. Sew an A triangle to the top. Sew the resulting triangle to the top of the shorter pieced strip; sew the entire piece to the top of the remaining strip. Sew this piece to a large white triangle along the diagonal to form a square.

Following the quilt block, sew an A triangle to one short end of a Pink strip; sew to the bottom of the large pieced square. Repeat with the second strip and triangle; sew to the right-hand side of the square. Sew on the smaller Pink triangle to complete. Clipping and notching

BASKET QUILT BLOCK   SCALE: 1 SQUARE = 1 INCH

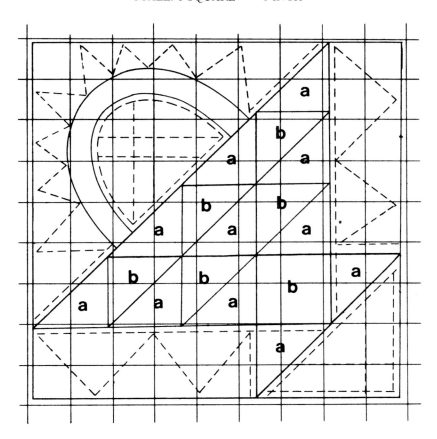

as needed, press under the seam allowance on handle. Applique in place. Trace quilting lines (broken lines) onto the block.

To assemble, arrange the blocks following Diagram A. Stitch the blocks together in diagonal strips; stitch strips together. Trim the edges of the quilt top. Sew on the side, then the top borders. Sew the side backing panels to center panel. Assemble the three layers following the directions above. Quilt each basket block along the traced lines; quilt plain blocks in diagonal lines 1¼ inches apart, forming diamonds. Turn ¼-inch of the backing and quilt top to the inside; slip stitch edges together.

To assemble the quilt, lay the backing flat on the floor wrong-side-up and arrange the batting over it. Lay the quilt top in place, right-side-up. Starting at the center of the quilt, baste out to the mid-point of all four edges. Then, starting at the center, baste to the four corners.

You'll now have basting in a star pattern. Trim the excess batting and baste around the outer edges.

To quilt by hand, place the quilt in a frame or loop. Use a short needle and short lengths of quilting thread and pull the knot through to the batting. Place the forefinger of your left hand over the spot where the needle should come through. With your right hand, push the needle through the quilt from below until it touches your finger. Pull the thread through with your right hand—your left forefinger is now put under the quilt. With your right hand, push the needle down through the quilt to touch your forefinger. Pull the thread through with your right hand. Continue working in this fashion. Fasten the end of each thread securely by running it between the layers.

To quilt by machine, use a long stitch (8-10 stitches per inch), and stitch along the quilting lines.

198

Damaged quilts and even quite small scraps of fabric can still be put to good use as cushion covers.

Here, a Texas quilt has been hung as a curtain to insulate a breezeway, right.

A valued Whig Rose quilt from Kentucky, brightens this apartment dining area, far right, and is displayed to full advantage.

Caring for Quilts

Caring for Quilts

Whether a quilt is inherited, homemade, or bought, it represents a valuable sentimental and monetary investment. Quilts, though once everyday items, deserve special care.

Many quilts are best appreciated when hung on a wall. If a quilt is in reasonably good condition, there is no reason why it can't be safely hung. The ideal spot would be one away from drafts, moisture, abrupt changes in temperature, and direct light, especially sun. Quilts can be very fragile and it is a good idea to give a hanging quilt a rest—perhaps displaying it in winter and storing it in summer, when bright sun and high temperatures are more likely to damage it.

Before choosing a method of display, take a close look at your quilt. Examine the pieced and appliqued seams: the stress of hanging will tend to further weaken any seams that are already coming apart. Also check to see that the quilting is strong. The quilting stitches that keep the batting from shifting also hold your quilt together, and assume a great deal of its weight when hung. If any of the stitching is loose or has come undone, repair the quilt before hanging.

In many pieced quilts, some of the fabrics may be ripped or worn away and before hanging those places should be professionally reinforced with similarly colored nylon net for protection. In the case of delicate quilts or quilts in which deterioration has already begun, consult a professional—museum textile departments can often supply references or suggest alternative methods of displaying a fragile quilt.

If the quilt is strong enough to withstand hanging, choose one of the following methods. If the quilt is heavy, it can hang from a wooden dowel. If the piece is lighter, use Velcro® to attach it to the wall and to hold it straight. Quilts with delicate backings of silk or other light fabrics should first have a muslin backing sewn over the real backing before utilizing either of these methods. Never pin nor staple a quilt to the wall

through the quilt top itself—the pressure of holding itself up will eventually tear the fabric.

To hang the quilt from dowelling you will need some tightly woven, medium- to heavyweight muslin, strong cotton thread, and wood dowelling. The dowel should be strong enough to support the quilt's weight, generally a 1- to 1¼-inch diameter is sufficient, and should be about 4 inches longer than the top of the quilt.

To make the sleeve, cut a muslin strip 1 inch longer than the quilt top, and wide enough to fold generously around the dowel plus about 3 inches. Turn the short ends of the sleeve under about ½ inch and press with an iron. Fold the sleeve in half lengthwise and press. Working on the back of the quilt, open the fold and pin the lower half of the sleeve to the quilt. Sew along the fold line using backstitches spaced about ½ inch apart, penetrating all quilt layers except the front. Be sure to make the stitches long enough so that they will not rip the quilt back, and loose enough so that they will not pucker. After sewing along the fold line, fold the upper part of the sleeve back down over the lower half, turning the bottom edge under about ½ inch. Using a catch stitch, sew the lower edge through all layers except the quilt front. These stitches form two rows that relieve the stress caused by hanging. Insert the dowel through the sleeve and support it on the wall with brackets. If desired, you can attach finials to the ends of the dowel to make it look more decorative.

If the wall behind the quilt is of unfinished wood or has areas where the paint has chipped away, it should be covered with an old sheet or muslin so that the quilt is protected.

With the Velcro method, the quilt's upper edge is more flexible and can be adjusted, which may be advantageous if the quilt has warped. Buy enough Velcro, at least 2 inches wide, to run along the length of the top, sides and bottom. Cut strips of Velcro about 6 inches long, enough to go around the edge of the quilt at 3-inch intervals. By hand or machine, sew both edges of the fuzzy half of the Velcro to pieces of muslin the same length and at least 2 inches wider, centering the Velcro on the muslin. Fold the muslin edges under so that ½ inch of muslin shows beyond the Velcro. Then pin the muslin and Velcro strip, fuzzy side up, along the top of the quilt back and attach as described for the sleeve.

Attach the rough side of the Velcro tape to the wall or to a muslin-covered board that will be hung on the wall with a staple gun. Hang the quilt by pressing the Velcro sides together firmly. From time to time, the Velcro will need to be re-pressed to keep it firmly in position.

When taking the quilt down for a rest, keep it in your own living conditions; the heat of the attic or dampness of the basement will accelerate deterioration. Ideally, a quilt should rest in a dark, airy, roomy space. Unfortunately, many quilts are stored wrapped in plastic bags, laid on closet shelves with mothballs, or folded in chests. Plastic bags trap dust and moisture, which may lead to mildew and mold; the chemicals in mothballs may damage the quilt's fibers; and the oils in pine or cedar chests are damaging to fine textiles.

Curators suggest wrapping quilts in cotton sheets or pillowcases, which will absorb any wood oils of boxes, chests, or shelves before they can penetrate the quilt. Unlike plastic, cotton allows the quilt to breathe, preventing mildew while protecting against dust. The quilt should rest with as little tension on its fibers as possible. Rolling is preferred; if space is at a premium, loosely fold the quilt over a clean cotton sheet so that it doesn't crease. Do not fold on a previous crease, tear, or any other wear mark, and refold the quilt frequently in a different way each time.

Quilts should be aired every six months. You can simply lay them flat on the floor for five days or so, in a room protected from foot traffic, or air them outside in the shade, when the weather is warm and dry.

To clean a quilt, the least disruptive method is to vacuum it through a fiberglass screen (available at hard-ware stores) whose edges have been bound with cotton twill. If the quilt has dirt marks or brownish streaks or circles, it needs a bath. The brown areas are acid from wood storage boxes or shelves, and left to itself an acid stain, or "agemark," will spread over the entire quilt.

Quilts must be wet-cleaned to remove acid and dirt. NEVER use a machine. Wet-cleaning should be done very carefully, for its effects can be irreversible: if a quilt fades in washing, it will be faded forever. For this reason, you should color test every single fabric in the quilt. It may take as long to color test a Log Cabin quilt as to wash it.

To color test, rub a clean, dry, white cloth gently over each fabric in the quilt, checking to see whether any color comes off on the cloth. If not, test each fabric three more times: first by dampening the cloth with cool water from the faucet, then with warm water, and finally with warm water and the washing agent—either Orvus paste or Woolite. Orvus is a natural product, and Woolite will wash out of the quilt thoroughly.

If the tests show that the colors will fade, do not wash the quilt. Instead, consult a textile conservator. If every fabric in the quilt passes the test, use lukewarm water and the washing agent, greatly diluted. Fill the bathtub first, as water should not run onto the quilt fibers. Rest the quilt in a sling made from fiberglass screening, and gently lower it into the water to soak for a few minutes. If the water turns yellow, it has become acidic and you must remove the quilt at once.

Repeat the wash using fresh water, then rinse the quilt, lowering the water temperature each time, until the water looks clean enough to drink. This may take eight to fifteen rinses. After the final rinse, press the quilt against the bottom of the tub to remove excess water, and roll it in an old cotton mattress pad or towels.

The quilt should dry flat, either outdoors in the sun to bleach the white fabrics and to kill whatever eggs might have been laid in the batting by pests, or indoors if you want to protect against fading. With fans overhead most quilts dry overnight, and others in two days or less.

Linens & Lace

*T*his dreamy bed shows several ways to give new linens an old look: sew lace to pillow shams, pillowcases, sheets, duvet covers, placemats, and napkins. Trims range from fanciful frills on the large shams to subtly elegant eyelet on standard pillows.

An antique sewing basket overflows with towels and napkins that have been extravagantly adorned.

The delicate colors and careful handwork of antique linens speak of gentler times long gone by. Unfortunately, though, not everyone has a grandmother or aunt with a trunk crammed with antique tablecloths, napkins, sheets, and pillowcases. And the prices of many antique linens are prohibitive.

But no matter. With a little patience and imagination, you can add a nostalgic touch to bed and bath, living and dining rooms. Rescue old lace borders from ripped or worn pieces or buy lace new and stitch it to shams, placemats, towels, sheets, or anything else you can think of.

Linens & Lace

INSTRUCTIONS

Here are instructions for a mix of linens and laces that may inspire you to embellish your own pieces. It is not necessary to exactly reproduce the linens photographed, but sewing tips follow for the items shown to give you the variety of techniques used.

Materials

Any variety of lace—new or antique, plain or lavish—can adorn linens. When choosing lace trims, measure each item and allow a few inches extra. Of course, older laces should be gently washed first. Sewing notions are by J. & P. Coats, including the thread for the machine embroidery and monogrammed initials—Dual Duty PLUS Extra Fine for lightweight fabrics and machine embroidery; machine embroidery hoop; monogrammed initials, dressmaker's tracing kit; Comforter Cover—two flat, queen-sized sheets, 25 yards of ¾-inch lace, Dual Duty PLUS Cotton Covered Polyester Thread for all fabrics (for seams), 10 yards of white bias corded piping, fabric marking pen with disappearing ink.

Sewing

Measure items where they are to be trimmed. Add extra inches for mitered or pleated corners, and 1-inch for each seam and end to be finished.

For each item, measure and cut the lace to the lengths needed, adding extra for finishing ends, joining seams, and pleating corners. The top edge of some laces is unfinished. Press this edge to the wrong side to form the desired width, and trim the edge to ⅜-inch. Stitch the lace to the linen using the machine's straight stitch or a machine-embroidery pattern as indicated.

For monogrammed initials, draw script initials on tissue paper and transfer them to the fabric using light color tracing paper from the dressmaker's tracing kit and a sharp, hard-lead pencil. Monogramming is done by machine using freehand embroidery and the machine-embroidery hoop (which holds the fabric flat against the machine's bed). For details on how to monogram, refer to the machine's manual or your favorite sewing book.

Sewing Tips

Pillowcases and sheets: Do the monogramming (1-inch high initials) before attaching the lace. Prepare the lace and pin it to the cases and sheets with the pressed edge extended just over the hemline; then stitch close to the pressed edge.

Comforter cover: Finished size is 88-by-90 inches. The cover described is for a queen-size comforter. For other sizes, buy two flat sheets in that size and adjust the lace and piping yardage as needed. On the right side of one sheet, mark diagonal lines from the corners as shown in the diagram. Mark the guide lines for the center rectangle A to measure about 13¼-by-15½-inches. Mark the lines for four more rectangles, spacing them the distance apart shown in the diagram. Center lace over the guide lines and pin or baste it in place. Stitch the lace along both edges. Stitch piping around the sheet ½-inch from the edge or just beyond the selvage, rounding corners. Place the two sheets with right sides facing, pin, and stitch around the edge just beyond the piping stitching line. Leave openings where shown in the diagram. Turn to the right side and press. Insert the comforter through the top opening and pull to the bottom through the side openings.

Neckroll: Pin the lace around each end with the edge projecting 1-inch beyond the neckroll end. Stitch the lace along the inner edge.

Ruffled shams: Lap edge of the ruffle over the crocheted trim and stitch close to the edge.

Tailored sham: Baste the lace over the sham so that it overlaps the edge by ½-inch, pleating the lace at sham corners. Machine embroider over the lace edge, selecting a stitch pattern that enhances the lace pattern.

Tailored sham: Prepare lace so that it measures 3⅜-inch wide. Pin the lace around the edge of the sham with scallops projecting beyond the edge, mitering the corners as you work. Machine embroider as for the sham above.

Boudoir pillow cover: The inner seam and edge of the flange are trimmed with lace. Prepare the lace and pin it over the inner seam, pleating it around the corners. Stitch along the straight edge of the lace. For the flange end, prepare the lace so that it measures ¾-inch wide. Lap the flange edge over lace and stitch.

Napkins and placemats: Lap the lace over the edge of the linen, mitering the corners. Stitch along the edge of the lace. Monogram an initial (1¼-inches high) in the corner of each napkin.

Guest towels: Pin a crocheted trim to the end of a towel, finishing the ends. Stitch along the straight edge of the lace, placing two rows ¼-inch apart.

Guest towels: Pin the lace to the towel and stitch as for the towels described above, with one row of stitching.

Jacquard napkins: Prepare the lace and machine embroider over the edge, with the satin-stitch pattern.

Placemats: Follow the instructions for the placemats described above.

Pillowcases: Baste lace over the end of pillow and machine embroider the edge with the scallop-stitch pattern.

COMFORTER COVER

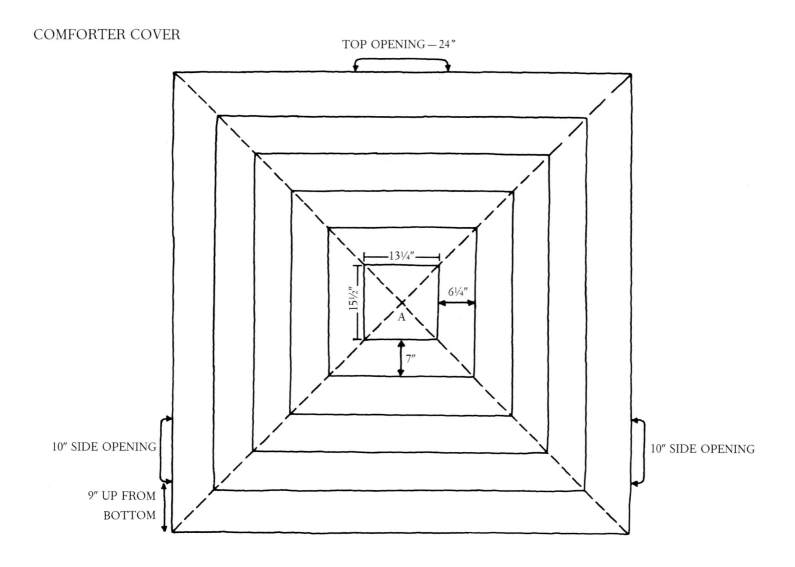

Cross-stitch

The sampler, napkin, and pillow shown opposite were all worked with counted cross-stitch on special even-weave needlework fabrics.

One of the easiest and most popular embroidery stitches, cross-stitch can decorate or monogram samplers, wall hangings, and table and bed linens, adding a personal touch to everyday items. At one time, cross-stitch samplers were made by every American schoolgirl to display her needlework skills and her mastery of the ABC's and 1-2-3's. Antique samplers commonly included the alphabet, numbers, and quotations from the Bible or popular verse, with pastoral scenes, houses, or various decorative elements to enliven the design and fill in empty spaces. That the sampler was a highly personal creation allowing a young woman to express herself perhaps accounts for much of its enduring charm for both creators and collectors. Samplers had strong sentimental value for their makers, and were often handed down to a dear relative or friend. Nowadays samplers are one of the most popular country arts, garnering high praise and high prices from collectors.

Hannah Crandal worked her 1809 sampler, above, in cross-stitch.

Cross-stitch

INSTRUCTIONS

Counted cross-stitch is usually worked on even-weave fabrics. These fabrics have the same number of threads in both directions, and, when cross-stitched, the resulting stitch will be square and uniform in size. Even-weave fabrics are available in different sizes and stitch counts (the number of stitches that can be worked on one inch of fabric). The stitch count determines the size of the finished design—the higher the count, the smaller and more detailed a design is possible.

Counted cross-stitch can also be worked on fabrics that do not have an even weave. In this case, waste canvas is basted over the fabric to facilitate counting and to obtain uniform stitches. Instructions for using waste canvas are given under Kitchen Towel with Chicken Motif information.

Working the Cross-stitch

Work the design following the chart; each square on the chart equals one stitch. The design is usually worked from left to right and in horizontal rows as shown in Diagrams 1 and 2. However, depending on the design, you may want to work one complete stitch at a time, such as for random, scattered stitches. Cross-stitch can also be worked vertically one stitch at a time, or in vertical rows.

DIAGRAM 1

DIAGRAM 2

To begin cross-stitching, let the thread end hang one inch on the wrong side of the fabric. Hold the end in place so that the first few stitches are worked over it, securing it in place. Cut the excess thread end after securing it. To end a thread, secure it by weaving through several stitches on the wrong side of the item; take a back stitch or two and cut the thread.

Schoolhouse

The schoolhouse motif is included for you to use as desired. It is worked on white Hardida Cloth No. 1481/1/55, a special needlework fabric woven in alternating squares of 11- and 22-count, which is a good fabric for tablecloths and pillows. The photograph on the previous page shows the schoolhouse worked on the 11-count squares in cross-stitch using three strands of floss.

SCHOOLHOUSE MOTIF

Kitchen Towel with Chicken Motif

Materials: A woven cotton or linen kitchen towel similar to that shown in the photograph; ¼ yard of waste canvas, 12-count, 510/48/27. Also, three skeins of Coats & Clark Royal Mouline Six-Strand Embroidery Floss, Color No. 2405 red; J. & P. Coats Tapestry Needle; Red Heart Sure-Hold Embroidery Hoop (optional).

Kitchen towels are usually not made of even-weave fabrics; the count and threads are irregular and fine, making counting for cross-stitching difficult. For our towels, the cross-stitch was worked over waste canvas, which was basted over the towel to facilitate counting and to obtain even, uniform stitches.

For the kitchen towel, cut a piece of canvas 6½ inches high. The length of your canvas should be 1 inch wider than the towel. Pin the canvas to one end of the towel, with one long edge of the canvas even with the towel's end, and canvas edges projecting ½ inch on either side of the towel. Baste the canvas to the towel horizontally and vertically.

Separate the floss and use four strands for stitching.

Following the chart, center and work the chicken design in cross-stitch over the waste canvas, and through the towel, using one square on the canvas to equal one square on the chart. Position the baseline of the design 1½ inches from the towel's end and work line to side edges.

When the design is completed, dampen the canvas with a clean sponge. Then, pull out the canvas threads one by one.

Alphabet Sampler

Materials: A 17-inch square of Pearl Aida cloth, 11-count, No. 1007/1/43, Color No. 1 white; five skeins of Coats & Clark Royal Mouline Six-Strand Embroidery Floss, Color No. 2405 red; J. & P. Coats Tapestry Needle; Red Heart Sure-Hold Embroidery Hoop (optional).

Using basting threads in a contrasting color, mark the horizontal and vertical center lines on the cloth square to correspond to the center guide lines on the chart. Overcast the edges. Separate the floss and use three strands for stitching. Work the design in cross-stitch, following the chart. Frame the sampler as desired.

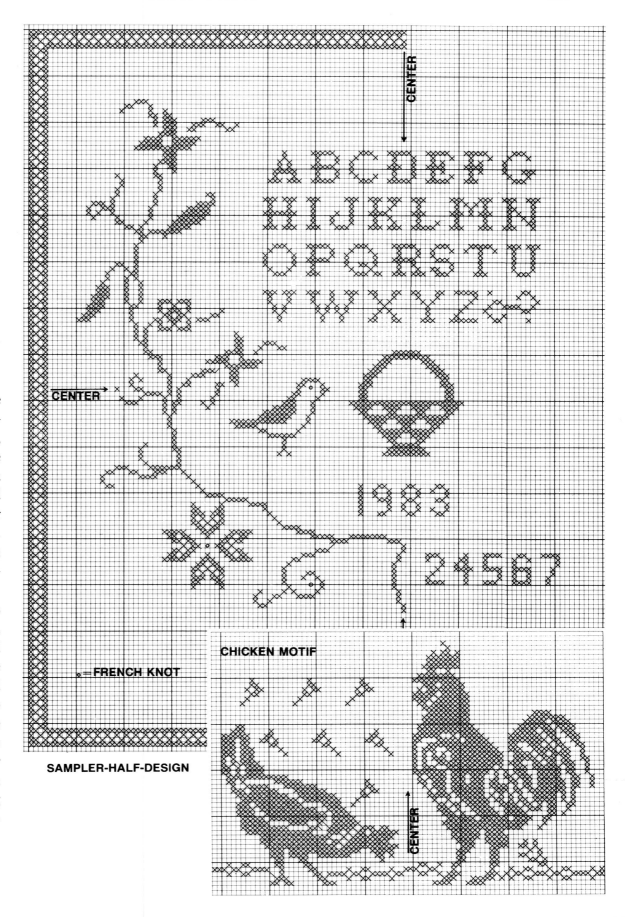

SAMPLER-HALF-DESIGN

∘= FRENCH KNOT

CHICKEN MOTIF

A Candlewick Bedspread

*W*hite-on-white em-
broidered candlewick
bedspreads originated in the
Blue Ridge Mountains in
the early nineteenth century.
The cotton candlewick was
worked by hand on bleached
muslin in various stitches,
most commonly the Colonial
or French knot.

A Candlewick Bedspread

In their quiet and imaginative determination to improvise simple beauty from the meagre materials available to them, Appalachian farm women created candlewicking. So called because it used as embroidery thread the same cotton cord used to make candlewicks, candlewicking was done on bleached muslin flour sacks sewn together to form a bedspread. Because the bedspread's pattern was usually transferred from an old spread, candlewick designs are almost unchanged over generations.

A candlewick bedspread is made by stretching the new spread material over an old spread and rubbing it with a cloth dipped in bluing solution until the pattern from the old spread appears on the muslin. This tracery is then covered with knots of candlewick, called Colonial or French knots, and the edges are fringed with more of the wicking. However, the following instructions will show you how to create your own pattern from scratch.

The finished spread is 86-by-102 inches excluding the fringe. Materials: J. & P. Coats Candlewick yarn (50-yard ball): 28 balls of No. 256 Natural; Red Heart Wooden Quilting Hoop, 14-inch diameter; J. & P. Coats Chenille needle Size 20; Coats & Clark Fabric Marking Pen. You will also need a size C crochet hook; an awl; 6 yards of heavy unbleached muslin or linen 54 inches wide; freezer paper; and a black marking pen.

To assemble the bedspread, do not preshrink the fabric. Cut the fabric in half widthwise to form two pieces, each 54-by-108 inches. Cut one piece in half lengthwise to form two pieces each 27-by-108 inches. The 54-by-108-inch piece is the center panel; the remaining pieces are for the side panels. With selvages together and making ½-inch seams, sew one long edge of each side panel to one long edge of center panel to form the bedspread. Press seams open. Fold the bedspread in half lengthwise and press the fold lightly. Then fold widthwise and press lightly. Where folds cross will be the center point of the bedspread.

Enlarge the design. The drawing shows half of the entire design. Join freezer paper to form a 46-by-108 inch piece. With a pencil, make a 1-inch grid on freezer paper, making the same number of squares as on the drawing. Mark a * on the grid and line it up to match the * on the drawing. Draw the design of each square of drawing onto the corresponding square on the freezer paper; then draw over all the lines of the design and outer cutting line with bold black marker.

Turn the freezer paper over and mark lines on the back of the paper as before. Matching the * on the enlargement with the center point of the spread, place the spread over the enlargement and pin in place. With a fabric marking pen, trace the design onto the spread, including the outer cutting line. This completes half of the design.

To transfer the other half of the design, turn the enlargement over and place under the spread, matching the * of the drawing with the center point of the spread. Pin in place and trace the design on the other half of the spread. This completes the entire design.

COLONIAL KNOT

1. WRAP THREAD AROUND NEEDLE ONCE.

2. WRAP THREAD AGAIN IN A FIGURE-8.

3. HOLDING TENSION ON THREAD, INSERT NEEDLE IN FABRIC NEAR POINT WHERE THREAD CAME UP; PULL THREAD TO PULL BACK.

To sew the candlewick, use the full four strands of yarn throughout, working with 18-inch lengths. Starting at the center of the spread, and using the hoop to keep the fabric taut, work Colonial Knots (see Stitch Detail) along all design lines, spacing knots ¼ inch apart. Work twelve knots for the perimeter of each grape. To prevent shadow-through, do not carry the thread across un-worked areas.

To hem, cut the spread along the cutting lines. Make a ½-inch hem around the spread, mitering the corners. Press the hem.

Fringe is worked along one long edge, lower edge and other long edge only, leaving the top edge free of fringe. Using the fabric marking pen and working on the wrong side of the spread, make dots along the hem-line ¼ inch in from the edge and 2 inches apart. Using an awl and starting at the upper corner, make a hole at each dot on the hemline.

Row 1: Cut six lengths of the 4-strand candlewick yarn, each 24 inches long. Fold strands in half to form a loop. With the right side facing you, insert the crochet hook from back to front in the hole and draw loop through; draw loose ends through the loop and pull tightly to secure, forming a "knot." Secure strands in each hole along all three edges. Row 2: Pick up half the strands of first knot and half the strands of second knot and knot them together 1 inch down between the twenty-three previous knots (see Fringe). Pick up remaining strands of previous knot and first half of strands of next knot and knot them together as before. Repeat from * along all three edges. Row 3: Using twelve strands for each knot, make another row of knots 1 inch down and in line with knots of Row 1. Trim the fringe.

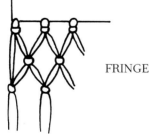

FRINGE

Laundering and pressing: First rinse the bedspread in cold water to remove the markings made by the fabric marking pen. Then after the marks are completely removed, wash in warm water and spin dry on gentle cycle. Spread out on a large sheet or blanket to dry. To press, place a plush towel on the ironing surface. Press the bedspread lightly with the right side down, using a steam iron. Be careful not to press the knots flat.

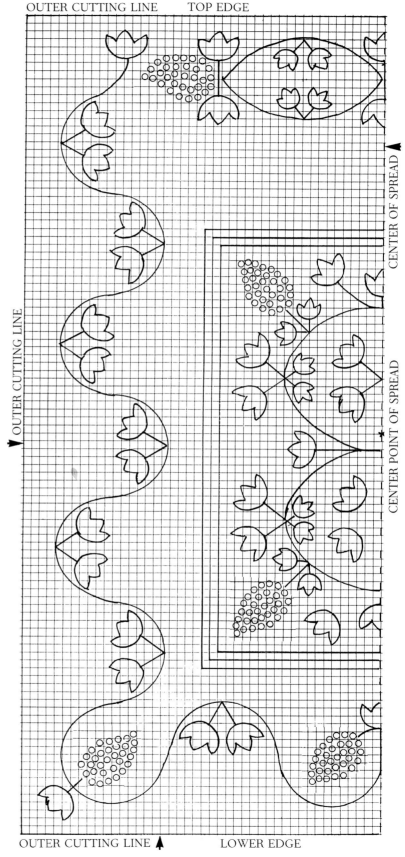

SCALE: 1 SQUARE = 1 INCH

*T*he rich, deep colors of milk paint and the imaginative faux marbre *design* create an authentic setting for the venerable portrait at left. The very thin single layer of paint on the door gives the impression of years of wear, and a black milk paint undercoat on the table adds depth. Both marbling and combing techniques have been used on the floor.

*R*andom combing on the table at top right creates a subtle effect appropriate for less formal furniture. Nicks and scratches only add to its appeal.

A skilled painter has marbled the four-poster bed at bottom right. The use of clean, light colors gives a contemporary look in perfect keeping with the house quilt and bedroom furniture.

Country Paint Techniques

Country Paint Techniques

Decorating with paint is a marvelous and often very easy way to transform even the starkest modern apartment into rooms alive with color and interest. Paint techniques such as stippling, sponging, dragging, and marbling can define a space, add architectural interest, or create an entire mood as a backdrop for country antiques and collectibles. These techniques with paint are almost infinitely adaptable, and many can be undertaken by someone with little or no experience. The more ambitious might want to comb a pattern on a floor, or attempt a trompe l'oeil effect, while those with less time can begin with a small picture frame or fireplace mantelpiece.

Because paint techniques can be used almost anywhere, from structural elements like walls and floors to moveable and built-in furniture, to small objects such as boxes and picture frames, you can experiment with all sorts of moods and color combinations. While larger spaces or built-in furniture might call for subtler effects, a small picture frame in pinks and blues makes a pretty addition to a baby's room. Inexpensive five-and-dime frames can be made to look like expensive antiques by using milk paints with a black undercoat, or by creating a tortoiseshell look with various brown hues.

Unremarkable or damaged chairs and tables picked up at flea markets are suddenly happy additions to a kitchen, porch, or child's room when painted white and sponged in bright primary colors, or combed to look elegantly "distressed." Cupboards painted with milk paint and perhaps a trompe l'oeil scene are worthy of one's favorite pottery or quilt collections.

Trompe l'oeil, strictly speaking, should look realistic, and this requires an artist's hand and eye. But there's no reason why the amateur shouldn't attempt more primitive trompe l'oeil effects, utilizing the naiveté of the painting technique as an integral and central part of the picture's charm. Working from a clear photograph or even from life, an ambitious painter can achieve unique effects which echo the artless simplicity of some of the colonists' work. Another means of achieving a trompe l'oeil effect is to mass stencils together to create a detail or even a whole painting, with the stencil replacing artistic skill.

Most paint techniques involve applying a thin coat or coats of paint with an instrument of some kind to create a random or repetitive pattern. The secondary color is instrumental in the finished effect and the greater the contrast the more intense the design will appear. The paint of choice for the overcoat is generally a glaze; an oil paint thinned with equal parts linseed oil and turpentine, or a water-based paint thinned with water, will each achieve a delicate, semi-transparent color wash that dries quickly and gives a smooth, luminous finish. Glazes can be store-bought or custom-mixed, the former offering ease and certainty, the latter less risk of a gummy effect, especially with more intense colors when the amount of color can thicken the glaze too much. Most of the books specifically on paint techniques will offer recipes for hand-mixed glazes.

A clean painting surface is one of the first requirements for a satisfactory final effect. Walls and woodwork should be cleaned of dust and grime with a sponge soaked in a mild detergent solution with a little ammonia, and sponged again with clean water to remove any traces of soap. Small cracks or holes in woodwork or plaster should be filled.

Paint walls with a standard undercoat, or primer, for the best finish. Once you have a base coat, you can rub it down lightly with fine sandpaper over a block of wood, vacuuming up the dust after, to get an absolutely perfect painting surface. In general, ceilings should be painted first, then walls, then woodwork.

Colorwashing

Colorwashing is literally applying a very thin coat of color over a creamy white basecoat in generous, random brushstrokes. This produces a watercolor effect perfect for country rooms and country furniture. The walls will look gently faded by time and sun, rather like the weathered pastel colors of many Mediterranean houses, and will reflect a warm, soft light onto the surrounding room.

For the glaze, use a heavily thinned matte oil or latex paint. Thin in a ratio of nine to one: nine parts thinner to one part paint, using mineral spirits for the oil and water for the latex paint. This is an economical mixture, and a little glaze will go a long way.

The procedure is extremely simple. Over the base coat, apply a thin coat of color with a wide brush, working every which way, paying no heed to the direction of the brush stroke or evenness of application. It is this irregularity which gives colorwashing its appealing texture. After the first coat has dried, apply another coat in the same manner over the bare spots and some of the painted ones, to build up two thin, slightly overlapping transparent coats of color. This can be a somewhat messy job, as the paint is likely to run off the wall, and sometimes has to be persuaded to stick by applying it with a soft brush in spots, but the second coat of color makes the whole effect come together nicely.

Combing

Comb-painted finishes would sometimes be used in early American homes to decorate a wood floor or piece of furniture and perhaps to disguise plain or inexpensive materials. The wavy, irregular lines drawn in wet oil-based paint by a rubber comb can be varied or modified as preferred, producing anything from the appearance of bold wood grain to a more abstract fantasy finish.

Combs can be bought from art supply stores but you can also cut your own from heavy cardboard, plastic, or plywood. Color combinations are, of course, infinite, but unless a very bold result is wanted, it is probably best to begin with two shades of the same color rather than two contrasting colors.

Paint the wood in the base color and allow it to dry. Thin the top color by adding one part mineral spirits to three parts paint. Then brush a small area with the top color and comb through the paint in one direction, wiping excess paint off the comb after each stroke. The final effect is meant to be irregular, so the comb lines do not have to match exactly. On floors and larger areas, a tiled effect can be created by squaring off the surface and combing each square in a right-angle direction to its neighbor.

A plain, unremarkable wall and window are brought to life with unexpected burnt orange hues and a sponge technique, above. Here the base coat is a deep bright color, and the sponging has been applied intermittently for a spotted effect.

This trompe l'oeil rug requires little upkeep and adds a colorful and humorous note to the stairwell, at left. The naiveté of its style only adds to its charm.

*B*lue and yellow are a cheerful combination, and the gaiety of the colors is relieved by judicious use of white and a variety of subtle patterns. The cupboard and chest have been both sponged and combed; the basket vase has been stenciled and sponged, and milk paint was used throughout for a matte finish.

Country Paint Techniques

Dragging

The technique of dragging is one in which a thin glaze of paint (usually oil-based) is applied over an undercoat and while still wet "dragged" in one or several directions with a brush to let the undercoat show through. This simple technique produces a sophisticated effect appropriate to more formal rooms, and is especially nice as a background for artwork. A single color can be dragged over a white undercoat, or for a more striking appearance, two complementary colors can work together, using one as an undercoat.

Dragging is best done by two people, one to apply and one to drag the paint, as oil glazes dry quickly and the dragging needs to be done as soon as the paint is applied. The painter, using a 4- or 5-inch fine bristled brush, begins in a corner and starts brushing, sparingly, so that the paint doesn't run, an 18-inch-wide strip of paint vertically from top to bottom. As soon as the painter is about half-way down the wall, the dragger starts at the top and drags down through the newly applied glaze using another wide, fine-bristled brush, creating vertical pinstripes. Use gentle but firm pressure for the dragging, and don't be concerned if the lines occasionally waver or seem uneven — once the paint has dried and pictures have been hung, the overall effect will be smooth and warm.

When the dragger reaches the halfway mark, more or less, the painter should have begun the next vertical stripe, slightly overlapping the first stripe of paint, so the dragger can continue without interruption. It is important not to pause in between dragging or painting until you reach a corner or other natural break, because the thin glaze will dry quickly and any hesitation will leave clear lines of demarcation. If these do occur, use a rag dipped in thinner to release the paint. Wipe the dragging brush frequently so that it doesn't begin to put more paint on than it removes.

If this procedure seems difficult for a large wall area, practice first on a small area of woodwork, dragging in the direction of the grain.

Ragging and Sponging

Ragging and sponging refer to the instruments used to apply the coat of paint to a prepared wall, both of which produce a textured, patterned surface. Ragging produces a more textured effect, somewhat like fabric, and looks well in gentler pastel colors. Like dragging, it is done to the glaze after it is on the wall and is best accomplished with two people: one brushes the glaze over the undercoat and the second dabs a bunched up, lint-free rag into the glaze every which way so that the pattern does not appear too regular or deliberate. The rag will need to be wiped and rebunched occasionally so that it doesn't reapply paint. Once dry, any unevennesses will fade.

Sponging is best accomplished with a sea sponge in a manageable size. Dip the sponge in turpentine first, to soften it, then dab it into the glaze before applying it randomly over the wall, only slightly overlapping itself, to achieve a mottled, subtle effect.

With both these techniques, experimentation with color can produce unusual and striking results. The base coat need not be white, and with sponging, two or three different colors can be built up over one another for a deeper, more patterned surface. Different applicators — crumpled up plastic wrap instead of rags, or a finer versus a coarser sponge — produce quite different looks.

Milk Paint

One of the most traditional finishes, milk paint was used for everything from wall stencils to blanket chests. Made from milk mixed with pigment to form mellow, rich colors, milk paints were used originally to protect and disguise soft woods, and they have a beauty that ready-mixed paints rarely achieve.

Milk paint is available commercially, or you can mix your own, from equal parts buttermilk or skim milk, lime, and pigment, straining the mixture to get rid of any lumps. Beware that, although milk paint is easy to remove when wet, it's there to stay as soon as it dries, so clean the brushes thoroughly with soap and water before they dry.

Milk paint produces an instant antique look: the deep, matte colors seem as though they've been mellowed by the years, with all the sharp brilliancy of the pigment toned down. Milk paint also highlights wood grains, and when applied in layers, achieves a rich color that looks authentically old. Milk paint can be purchased through the resources on page 251.

Bleaching and Pickling

In old Scandinavian homes, assiduous homemakers regularly cleaned their wood floors with sand, rubbing the wet paste into the planks until, over the years, the floors were bleached to a pale, matte color. Bleaching and pickling achieve a similar effect, the first leaving the wood pale but unfinished, and the latter giving a raw floor a lighter look by introducing pale-colored paint into the unfinished open grain.

The process of bleaching literally takes the color or stain out of wood floors or furniture with a household bleach, sometimes preceded by a chemical stripper to remove any protective varnish. Pickling works well on oak and other open-grained woods, and is effected by brushing a sanded floor or stripped wood furniture with white or pale-colored thinned enamel paint and wiping it off, to leave paint only in the softer grain lines. Because these procedures require heavy sanders and chemicals, they are generally best left to professionals.

The stencil pattern on the floor, left, was copied from the nineteenth century Bump Tavern in Cooperstown, New York.

Above, a handmade frosted Mylar stencil, japan paints, and brushes await their next job.

The exuberant corner stenciling, top right, was based on a maple leaf design in an old book of New England stencils.

Bottom right, a lead-and-star design is shown.

The Art of Stenciling

Stencils provided a means for the country dweller of old to decorate walls, floors, and furniture with pleasing designs. Itinerant stencilers, equipped with popular stencil patterns, dry pigments, and brushes, travelled the countryside decorating rural homes in exchange for room, board, and a small fee.

Generally, old stencil patterns were taken from nature and depicted leaves, berries, flowers, birds, and animals in naturalistic or stylized designs. Because stencilers travelled wherever their services were needed, favorite patterns appeared all over the Northeast, to be traded among stencilers and reused by the same craftsman in many different homes. Today, reproductions of traditional designs are widely available but one of the endless pleasures of stenciling is that almost any kind of new pattern can be used.

Early American stencilers worked with milk paint, and this accounts for their deep matte colors: black, green, yellow, ochre, red, pink, and occasionally red-brown (blue was rarely used). The modern stenciler can choose from any variety of oil- or water-based paints, each of which produces a slightly different effect.

The Art of Stenciling

INSTRUCTIONS

These are general instructions for stenciling. The patterns reproduced on these pages can be the basis for a design on walls, floors, fabrics, or any stenciling project.

On floors, the stencil patterns can create a border, or they can be made to look like a rug if the interior area and a narrow surround are painted in a different color than the rest of the floor.

Stenciling can be as complicated or simple as you want. For more detailed instructions, and a host of both antique and modern designs, consult one of the numerous books on stencil design and techniques.

Very little paint is usually needed for stenciling, especially since a crisp, even outline is best achieved with a sparing application of color. Premixed oil-based paints, poster paints, or, in the case of wood surfaces, stains, can work successfully as long as the surface is primed to accept the paint. If water-based paint is selected, the color should be protected from washing off with a clear polyurethane finish.

Japan colors, though sometimes difficult to find, are recommended by many experts for stenciling on floors, furniture, and many other hard surfaces because they handle well and produce the finest shadings. Acrylic paints tend to produce either a completely opaque or a transparent finish and are more difficult to work with because they dry quickly and form a fine skin, so brushes need to be cleaned regularly while working. For a completely authentic look, milk paint can be bought commercially, or even mixed at home. Some experts do use spray paints, and you might experiment with these as well. Whatever medium you choose, take some time to practice on scrap paper until you've mastered the technique—clean lines, no running, fine shadings.

Stenciling brushes, of both synthetic and natural bristles, are round brushes with a flat applicator end and are necessary if you want to produce a professional result. They come in a variety of sizes, and you should have the 2-inch ones for larger stencils, as well as a variety of smaller sizes for details. Though natural bristle brushes are expensive, they will last a long time and are worth the expense. You should have a different brush for each color. Carpenters' gluing and rubbing brushes can be used for stencils, though they might be difficult to find. Stenciling brushes come in both long- and short-handled styles, and which you choose is purely a matter of comfort and preference.

For all stenciling, you will need:
sheets of Mylar® or Chronaflex®, from art supply stores
a no. 2 pencil
masking tape
an X-acto knife and blades
small, shallow dishes
paper towels
stencil brushes or blunt-end paint brushes
paint
turpentine or mineral spirits (for oil-based paints)

MOTIFS FOR WALL   SCALE: 1 SQUARE = ½ INCH

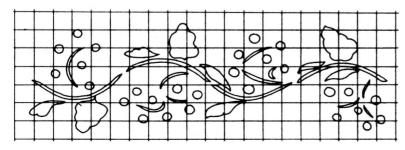
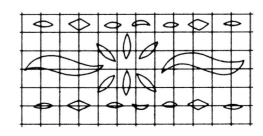

STENCILING GUIDELINES

To enlarge a motif for your patterns, either photocopy up to the larger size or draw a larger graphed background to the size preferred onto a piece of paper and copy the stencil pattern square by square.

To prepare the stencil, place Mylar or Chronaflex over the pattern and trace the outlines with a sharp pencil. If the stencil is to be painted in more than one color, cut a separate stencil for each color. On the pattern itself, assign each color a number and number the areas of the pattern that correspond to the colors.

Cut a piece of Mylar for each color, large enough to allow a 1-inch margin around the outside. Center the Mylar over the pattern and tape it in place. Trace only the parts labeled for the first color. Place a second piece of Mylar over the pattern and trace the areas for the second color. Trace the contours of shapes on the first stencil using a broken line to form a registration so the two will line up properly when painted. Continue in this manner for additional stencils if more colors are being used. Label each stencil.

To cut out, work on a hard smooth surface like a cutting mat or piece of glass backed with white paper so that you can see what you are doing. Using a sharp X-acto blade, work carefully, cutting towards yourself for better control. Cut the smaller design elements first and try to keep all edges as smooth as possible. On each stencil, cut out only the areas to be colored. Before applying paint, lightly mark the area to be stenciled with pencil guidelines. To prevent paint from smearing or running, tape the stencil firmly in place with masking tape and work with as dry a brush as possible. Pour a small amount of paint into a shallow dish. Dip the end of the brush gently into the paint and wipe off the excess on a paper towel. Press the stencil flat against the wall surface and apply the paint working from the outside in, using a light tapping motion, with the bristles meeting the surface head-on. Carefully lift the stencil away and wipe it clean.

Stencil one color at a time, covering the entire area to be stenciled; then, progress to the next color. Let the paint dry thoroughly between colors. For subsequent colors use the uncut outline of the first color areas to register the stencil.

MOTIF FOR FLOOR

SCALE: 1 SQUARE = 1 INCH

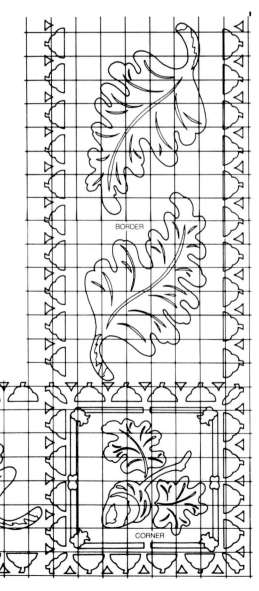

Penny Rugs

Copper pennies served as templates for the scrap fabric used to make this sixty-year-old hexagonal-shaped rug, left. On the chair back is an oval penny rug made from fabric tongues. Instructions for both these rugs are overleaf.

These penny rugs, most from Vermont and dating from the turn of the century, illustrate the varied patterns possible with this frugal technique by embellishing the pennies with embroidery or applique.

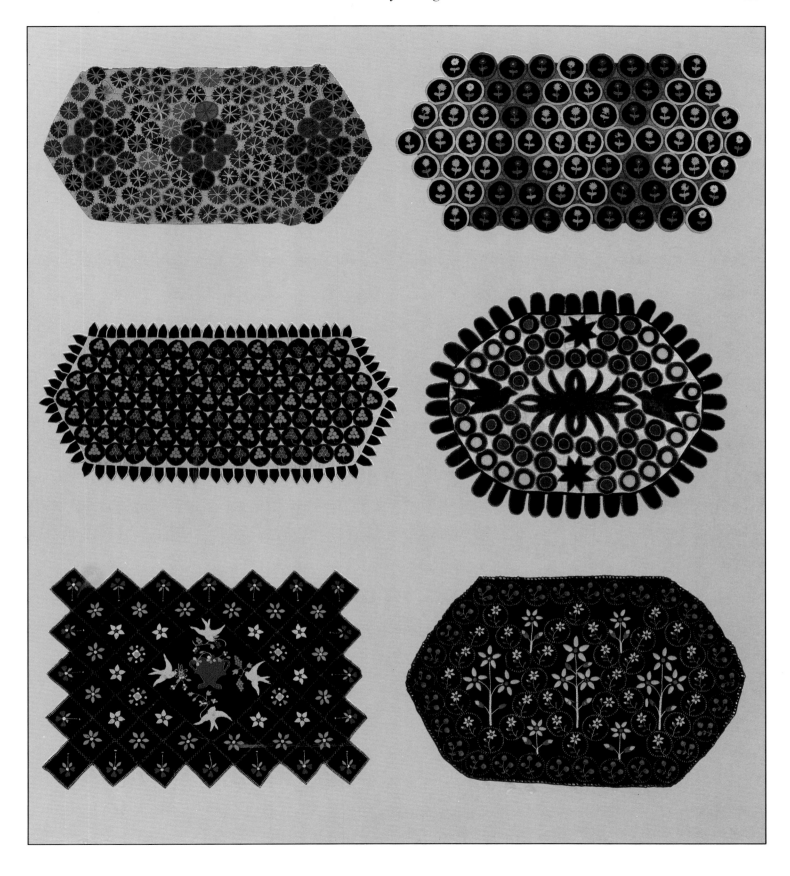

Penny Rugs

The large copper pennies used as the templates for cutting out the circles that made up these rugs earned them their interesting moniker. Made primarily in northern New England and Quebec, penny rugs were once as popular as hooked rugs, though they are less well-known today. They probably originated as projects designed to teach sewing skills, and much of their charm comes from the imaginative and highly individual designs created by their makers.

Penny rugs were often used as table covers, since they are not durable enough to withstand much foot traffic, though some may have served as scatter rugs in lightly travelled areas. The circles of felt were sewn to a felt background — usually black, to highlight the bright colors of the many fabrics and threads — and this was backed by burlap, often a burlap feed bag. The use of circles to create geometric patterns creates a dynamic, modern effect in the best penny rugs, wherein one pattern is most visible from far away, and then up close another predominates.

Penny rugs were decorated with embroidery and applique and often display figurative motifs from nature — naive representations of animals, birds, and flowers. The rugs photographed are decorated with the buttonhole stitch, which often functioned as an edge finish on circles and tongues. It also secured circles to the backing.

Choose the yarn type and color that will work best with your fabrics. Possibilities include six-strand cotton floss, single-strand pearl or matte cotton, or three-ply needlepoint yarn. If you use needlepoint yarn, separate and work with two plys.

There are no set rules for making a penny rug. Experiment with shape and color placement — an endless number of geometric patterns can be formed by combining colored circles. As you work, pin all the circles in place, then stand back to look at the composition before doing the final sewing. You may want to sketch and color your designs on paper before translating the final design into fabric.

After you have seen a number of penny rugs, you will learn to think in terms of circles and tongues when designing a rug. The rugs shown on the previous pages were formed with these simple shapes. Some rugs combine circles with a border of tongues. On others, a center area is left free of circles and embellished with embroidered and appliqued designs.

INSTRUCTIONS

A penny rug is constructed of three fabric layers: a top, a base, and a backing. For your rug, the top should be of felt or medium-to-heavyweight wool-type woven fabrics in solids, plaids, or stripes. For the base, use felt in a color that coordinates with the top fabrics, and for the backing, burlap, a heavyweight cotton, or linen-type fabric works best.

Choose fabrics that are tightly woven so that they won't fray — this is a good project for recycling worn clothing. First, machine-wash and dry clothes to tighten the weave and prevent fraying.

Hexagon Rug

The hexagon rug is formed by arranging and sewing circles, using a buttonhole stitch, to the felt base. A general approach for making a similar rug would be to cut out three circular templates of cardboard with diameters measuring 1 inch, 2 inches, and 2¾ inches. Using the templates, trace and cut out fabric circles in chosen colors. Each finished circle is a combination of three circles made as follows. Center and sew the small circle onto the medium-sized one. Then, center and join this to the large one. Make as many circles as you think necessary. More can always be made as you go along, so don't worry about having the exact number to begin with.

To assemble the rug, cut the felt base several inches larger all around than the finished rug size. Then arrange and pin the circles on the base, working from the center out. In the rug photographed, the circles are placed with edges overlapping, but they can also be arranged with edges just touching. Sew all circles except the outer row to the base. Trim away the excess base felt so the edges of the outer row of circles extend beyond it, as shown in the diagram, then sew the outer row of circles to the base and finish the extending edges with the buttonhole stitch. Pin the rug, right-side-up, onto the backing fabric and trim away the excess backing so that it extends a half inch beyond the edges of the base. Turn the backing edges under even with the edges of the base, and whip-stitch them together.

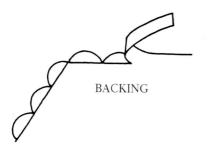

BACKING

Oval Rug

The oval rug is formed of overlapping rows of tongues. The following is a general approach for making one of these rugs. Again, before stitching the tongues in place, pin them in place to work out any adjustments.

To make the tongue shape, cut a cardboard template 2 inches wide and 3 inches long, and round one short end of the rectangle. With the template, trace and cut out fabric tongues in the desired color or colors. Finish the edges of the tongues with a buttonhole stitch and decorate each with lazy-daisy stitches (illustrated in any embroidery how-to book). If you wish to save time, embroider only the portion of the tongues that will show. A close look at the photograph will show that yarn colors vary from row to row.

To assemble the rug, cut the felt base about 1½ inches larger all around than the planned size of the rug. Pin a row of tongues around the edge of the base, overlapping it by about 1 inch. Machine-stitch the tongues to the base with two rows of stitches spaced about ½ inch apart near the square ends. Working toward the center, pin a second row of tongues to the base so they overlap the first row. Stitch the second row to the base. Continue adding rows until the felt base is covered. As you work toward the center, you may need to shorten the tongues by trimming the square ends which are butted together to form the next-to-the-last row. For the last row, cover the square ends of the preceding row with a single line of tongues. Pin the rug, right-side-up, on the backing, and finish in the same manner as the hexagon rug.

Hooked Rugs

Hooked rugs are the essence of country: modest materials combined with frugality and imagination to create objects of enduring beauty and utility. The transformation of scraps of rag into a colorful heirloom satisfies both our practical and our aesthetic sensibilities. More durable than penny rugs and more design-versatile than rag rugs, hooked rugs often depict scenes or objects from everyday life, as well as traditional design elements like flowers or geometric patterns. A contemporary hooked rug can utilize this time-honored form for contemporary expression. The instructions that follow show how to make the flower design at opposite top; once you've mastered the hooking techniques, it requires only your imagination to create any design.

Hooked rug designs can be very versatile and range from abstract patterns to figurative scenes.

Popular stencil patterns for hooking included a basket or urn of flowers, as in this wall-hung rug.

The instructions overleaf explain how to make the floral patterned Nottingham rug, left.

Most hooked rugs were intended as small area rugs; larger examples, such as below, are rarer.

Hooked Rugs

INSTRUCTIONS

Materials: a 30-by-40-inch piece of good-quality burlap (12–13 threads per inch); rug hook with a medium hook; dressmaker's carbon paper; a hard lead pencil; 3½ yards 1¼-inch-wide twill rug tape; embroidery hoop or frame for holding the rug taut while hooking; brown wrapping paper and tracing paper, both 25-by-36 inches. Fabrics: The original rug was hooked by designer Ruth Hall from a collection of old woven wool fabrics. The floral design was hooked in muted colored tweeds, checks, soft grayed rose shades, grayed greens, blues and golds; the background is of a creamy gold tweed (estimated amount: 1¼ yards); the border is of checks and tweeds.

If you have a collection of tweeds and other mixtures, you may be able to use them as is. Or, if you feel they are too bright, you can make the colors subtler by over-dying, which is dying fabric without first removing its original color. Overdye red and rose tweeds with a weak dye bath of khaki. If desired, overdye other colors also.

The wool strips must be cut exactly on the straight of the grain, or else they will pull apart as you hook. To ensure cutting them straight, tear the fabric into 3-to-4-inch-wide strips before cutting, and then cut these into at least ⅛-inch-thick strips parallel to the torn edges.

With a sewing machine, make two rows of stitching ¾ inch beyond the edge of the design, as shown in Diagram 1. Stitch rug tape around the edge of the design, easing it around corners.

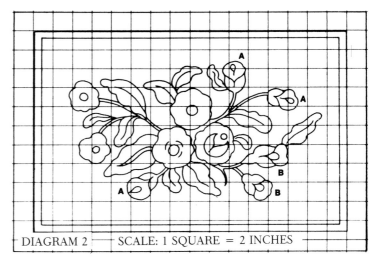

DIAGRAM 2   SCALE: 1 SQUARE = 2 INCHES

Use Diagram 2 to enlarge and transfer the design to your piece of burlap. Work on a large piece of brown wrapping paper, and starting with a perfect right angle at one corner, mark the paper in the same number of squares as shown on the chart—each square to be enlarged to the scale given under the diagram. Copy the pattern square by square. Now, trace the design on tracing paper. Center this copy on burlap and transfer it using the dressmaker's carbon and the hard lead pencil.

Begin the rug by hooking the three center roses, as shown in Diagram 3. Then do the surrounding leaves,

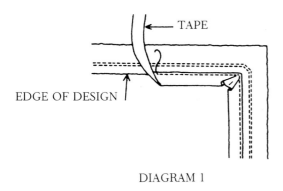

DIAGRAM 1

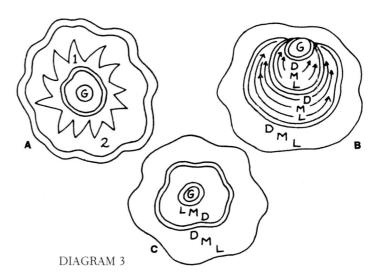

DIAGRAM 3

working out to the end flowers and leaves. Keep the roses flat, open, and simple; hook by following the flower outline. At first some loops will be higher than others, but your technique will improve with practice. Little irregularities will soon even out when the rug is on the floor, so don't worry about them.

The pattern should be in a frame to hold it taut. Hold the hook in your right hand above the pattern with a strip of wool in your left hand beneath the pattern. Push the hook through the burlap, sliding the small shank of the hook between the thumb and finger of your left hand, until it catches hold of the wool strip which is held between your thumb and forefinger, as illustrated

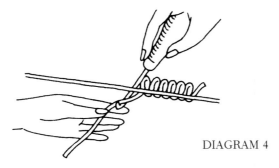

DIAGRAM 4

in Diagram 4. Pull up the strip, bringing the end through to the top side to a height of about an inch. All ends are brought to the top side and later trimmed to the same height as the loops. Now put the hook into the next mesh and pull up a loop about ⅛ inch. As you pull up, press the smooth side of the hook against the burlap to make the hole bigger so the hook can pass through easily. Working in any direction, keep pulling up the loops evenly, skipping a mesh occasionally to keep loops from being packed too tightly. They should touch each other comfortably. When the end of the strip is reached, bring it through to the top side.

Hook roses B and C using dull rose shades in about three values: a dark (D), medium (M), and medium-light (L). Use brown for outlining (double lines). For rose A, use several golds (G) in the center—a darker gold in the center spot surrounded by a lighter gold. Use two rows of a gray tweed for the double line surrounding the golds and outlining the flower. For the irregular radiating lines (l), use a red tweed, filling in area 2 with dull rose shades from flowers B and C.

Hook the two flowers at the end (in Diagram 5) as follows. Outline using a gold tweed, using a much darker tweed to outline half way (----); fill with medium gold tweeds using a line of lighter, brighter gold at (....). Use a blue-green tweed at center.

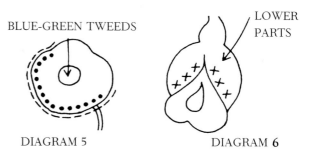

BLUE-GREEN TWEEDS

LOWER PARTS

DIAGRAM 5   DIAGRAM 6

Use green tweeds for the lower part, placing the darker ones along the outside edge and the lighter ones along x's. (See Diagram 6.) Fill buds marked A in Diagram 2 with dull rose tweeds; outline tear drop centers with contrasting tweeds, either a gold or dark red. Hook buds B in dull blue tweeds with a gold tweed center.

Hook the veins in either a red or gold check. Outline the leaves with a dark green or brown check. Fill the leaves with a variety of lighter green checks. On some, you may fill one side of a leaf with soft yellow greens, and the other side with dull blue greens. For the stems, use a variety of the same colors, placing darker greens in the center, lighter ones on the sides.

Hook three or four rows of creamy gold tweed around all motifs. Then fill in the remainder. If the background wool is a combination of several similar but different fabrics, some tweeds and some plain, cut strips and mix them up in a pile, and then hook them so that you ensure no pattern is being followed.

For the border, use dull tweeds and checks, hooking one row of greens, one of red, two in blue green, then about six in various reds. The final row or two should be hooked in gray-brown.

Using a damp cloth, steam press thoroughly on the wrong side, and again, lightly, on the right side. Trim the excess burlap beyond the two rows of stitching, and then hand sew the tape to the wrong side, mitering the corners. The tape, when turned back, should cover the excess burlap.

Dried Flowers & Potpourris

A summer potpourri includes bay leaves and rose petals and is displayed in an open wood bowl to release its fragrance throughout the home, top right. Opposite, a tableau of miniature pumpkins tied with dried grasses and autumn leaves is illuminated by thick tallow candles. At bottom right, a painted still life is reproduced with half-finished lemon pomanders and their spice curing mixture.

Scenting rooms with the delicate aromas of the outdoors, of pine and cinnamon in winter or the sweet summer scent of roses and cornflowers, conjures up the atmosphere of an old-fashioned home. With drying, flowers assume a new and different beauty. Colors mellow, perfumes deepen, and scents blend in original and highly idiosyncratic ways. A homemade potpourri or sachet can become one's personal trademark, a whisper of the presence of the maker that charms the household. Scented mixtures serve functional purposes as well: our ancestors had recipes that, among other things, drove away flies and moths, stimulated the sleepy, fumigated sickrooms, and assured pleasant dreams.

Dried Flowers & Potpourris

DRYING FLOWERS AND HERBS

Drying flowers, herbs, or any other botanical is an eminently simple affair, and requires only a gentle touch and some patience. In fact, most herbs and flowers can be hung to dry in a dark, dry, well-ventilated place. Different botanicals take different times and conditions, so experiment with environments for each.

When choosing flowers for drying, pick mature blooms, and as with any botanical, pick them when they are dry, after the morning dew or rain has evaporated. Always be careful not to bruise the leaves or flowers, and pick over and discard the brown or imperfect leaves and buds.

To hang dry, strip the first few inches or so of the stems and tie the flowers together with cotton string, using the end of the string to hang the bunch from a rafter, clothesline, or peg. You may want to slip a rubberband around the stems as well, in case they shrink so much in drying that they slip out of the string. If the drying room is not warm enough, flowers will lose their color, and if bunches are too big or hung too close together, the flowers will be misshapen and air will not circulate among the blossoms. You may want to experiment with drying places by hanging similar bunches in different rooms at the same time, and then compare drying times and color preservation later.

Grasses and flowers with heavy blooms such as full-blown roses, peonies, or dahlias can be dried flat on mesh screens or brown paper. You can also slip the stems of flowers through the mesh so that the blooms are supported upon the screen and not crushed on one side by laying flat. Another method of drying flower petals is to layer them in a plastic box with dry, clean sand or crushed silica gel (available at florists' supply shops), leaving them until they rustle like paper. This method preserves their color best of all, but be careful that flowers do not touch one another while drying.

Depending on the weather, herbs usually take about two weeks to hang dry, and flowers can take anywhere from a few days to a few weeks. Leaves and petals should be as dry as paper and twigs and stems should break, not bend.

To dry botanicals quickly, spread the scented leaves on a cheesecloth-covered rack or baking sheet in a 90°F oven. Leave the oven door open and stir the leaves occasionally until they are completely dry. Or, use a microwave to dry herbs. Thicker leaves take up to three minutes and smaller, drier leaves will be done in about one minute.

To dry flowers for an old-fashioned moist potpourri, start with partially dried rose petals. The partial drying retains more of the scented oils, and thus is more fragrant and longer-lasting, but it doesn't look as pretty as dry potpourri and so it is usually kept in a covered container that can be opened to release the scent.

In a wide-mouthed earthenware container alternate layers of kosher salt and flower petals and cover tightly. Stir the mixture once a day for about a month. As the level in the container drops, add more layers of flowers and salt. When the petals have dried completely, you can mix them with dried scented geranium leaves, herbs, other flowers, and citrus skins for a long-lasting potpourri. This type of potpourri should be kept in a covered container and opened when the fragrance is desired. Experimentation will reveal the best mixtures of scented botanicals.

Dry potpourris can be made from any combination of fragrant and colorful herbs, spices, and flowers. Cornflowers, roses, marigolds, and pansies add color, while bergamot, chamomile, carnations, lavender, syringa, and violet are among the botanicals that add fragrance. Good spices to try are allspice, cardamom, cinnamon, cloves, ginger, and mace. Scented leaves appropriate for dry potpourris include basil, bay, eucalyptus, lemon balm, myrtle, rose geranium, rosemary, tarragon, and thyme. To whatever combination you choose, add chopped orris root and gum benzoin, approximately one ounce per pound of potpourri, to help preserve the scent. Dried pieces of citrus peel, some studded with cloves, are a bright, fragrant addition to potpourri.

Potpourri can be wrapped up in prettily embroidered handkerchief or floral fabric tied with ribbon to make a sachet. Sachets scent drawers, closets, linen cupboards, trunks, or any other dark, dry place. They are particularly charming when tied to a doorknob or bedpost as a welcoming gesture to a guest. Special potpourri mixtures designed to induce sleep—which often include peppermint leaves, chamomile, and hops—can be sewn into small satin pillows and tucked behind a bed pillow for a soporific effect.

Tussie Mussies

In the nineteenth century, little bouquets of dried or fresh flowers and herbs were given as gifts between friends and lovers. By choosing botanicals with an eye to their meanings, the giver could send a special message with a tussie mussie. The recipe that follows would be appropriate for a new mother or a friend in the hospital, containing as it does thyme for bravery, lemon balm for sympathy, and basil for love.

Tussie mussies of dried flowers and herbs form a lasting and lovely token of affection. For one tussie mussie, you'll need a small bunch of yellow and white flowers, one bunch of thyme, one bunch of lemon basil, and some lemon bergamot, lemon balm, and whole, fresh-scented geranium leaves (lemon or rose would be appropriate). The tussie mussie also requires aluminum foil, a small paper doily, and about one foot of thin colored ribbon to finish the bouquet.

Arrange the flowers you've chosen in a small bunch. Daffodils convey regard, daisies innocence, honeysuckle devoted affection, lily-of-the-valley a return of happi-

ness, and roses love. Traditional tussie mussies always contain at least one rose.

Encircle the flowers first with the lemon thyme, then the basil, bergamot, and balm, forming four layers of herbs. Wrap the entire bunch with geranium leaves and wrap a doily around the nosegay so that the lace edge frills out around the geranium leaf border. You may want to cut a hole in the center of the doily.

Wrapping the stems with floral tape will make the tussie mussie more stable. Finally, tie a ribbon around the bouquet using a double knot to keep the flowers in place.

Pomanders

Pomanders—fruit studded with whole cloves, dried and then used to scent drawers, closets, and the like—are traditional Christmas ornaments, and can be hung in closets or tucked away in drawers (though they are too pretty to hide) all year long. A pomander can be made from any citrus fruit, usually an orange or a lemon, or from an apple.

To make a pomander, take an unblemished, firm piece of fruit and perforate the skin all over with a sharp instrument like an ice pick or a knitting needle, in no particular design but far enough apart that the cloves will fit. Press a whole clove into each hole, completely covering the fruit. Then roll the clove ball in a mixture of allspice, cinnamon, ginger, nutmeg, and orrisroot. Leave it to dry in a paper bag or other warm, dry dark place until it is hard. A pomander will last for years.

Wreaths

Awreath is a satisfying way to capture the fugitive beauty of fresh flowers and greens and preserve them for the cooler months. Though the traditional wreath is woven from sprigs of evergreen or holly, wreaths of dried herbs and flowers, of twisted vines and twigs, or of vegetables, leaves, and many other natural elements are all the more pleasing for their unexpectedness and are entirely at home in a country setting.

Wreaths require the same attention to color, texture, and shape as does any decorating project, and can be as simple as a twisted grapevine entirely unadorned or as colorful and romantic as balsam branches covered in dried flowers.

Heather, nutmeg, and cinnamon are part of this fragrant wreath, hung beside a linen cupboard to scent the heirloom quilts.

Purple heather composes the Valentine's wreath, top. Thick vines have been bent into shape for the wreath above. Small sprigs of white statice add a summer air.

The cornhusk wreath, top left, rewards painstaking work by becoming a permanent treasure. As a memento of a gardener's first harvest, perhaps, the wreath will give pleasure for years to come. The essence of simplicity, the russet wreath, above right, is made on a twisted coathanger with a string of dried red peppers. The shed door wreath, opposite, is decorated with a spray of dried grasses and flowers tied with a lavender ribbon. Eucalyptus is included for its cooling scent. A simple wreath like this one can support a constantly changing array of embellishments.

Wreaths

A wreath is an innovative way to utilize an overabundance of garden flowers and herbs, or to pay homage to the wildflowers and grasses that grow in a beloved place. The means by which the wreath-maker resolves these dilemmas is the purest expression of creativity and personal style. Hung on a door to welcome guests, on a wall to brighten a room, placed flat on a beautifully composed dinner table as a centerpiece or candle holder, given as a gift, or even worn as a hat to a garden party or wedding, a wreath is a simple and lasting celebration of the delights of country living.

INSTRUCTIONS

Because wreaths can be made of so many different things—flowers, herbs, grasses, leaves, twigs and vines, or any combination of these—these instructions are meant to be general guidelines. For unadorned twig or vine wreaths, that is essentially all you will need. For other types of wreaths the following items can be useful and most are available at floral supply supply stores or florist's shops:

straw or styrofoam forms and bendable wire
florist's pins and wire
floral tape
craft glue
clear floral fixative spray

Experience and a delighted eye are the best guide in choosing the plants to use, and you may want to experiment with wreath compositions to see how different elements work together before fixing them in place. The following list, though by no means exhaustive, is offered as a beginner's guide to the botanicals that work well in wreaths.

As background materials, the pale gray of Silver King and Silver Lace Artemisia work well, as do the various greens of pines, balsams, and spruces. Sea lavender provides a gray-lavender setting, spanish moss a gray-green, ferns a very summery green, and holly and ivy a particularly festive and textural look. Of course, any of these can be accent materials as well. Herbs that work well in wreaths include opal basil, parsley, rosemary, and sage, but practically any well-dried herb will contribute color, form, and fragrance. For scent and shape, eucalyptus is effective, and lavender offers its misty purple, warm perfume, and full buds. Heathers are also good choices for fullness and color. Grasses, when used in handfuls, are lovely and will reveal subtle colors not evident in single strands. Flowers of course, are the queens of wreaths, and can be used by the bud or by the bouquet. Flowers to be dried for wreaths should be chosen at the peak of their bloom, unless the small bud shape is specifically desired.

Flowers, herbs, and grasses need to be dried before they are made into wreaths, and this can be done in any dark, warm, dry, well-ventilated place—a large closet, an attic, or a barn are particularly good spots. Tying bunches to hang upside down is the simplest method of drying; botanicals can be dried upright, in any container that has a hole in the bottom so air can circulate.

Some delicate or heavy-blossomed flowers will need support when drying, which is achieved with a mesh screen: the stems can be dropped through the screen, so the blooms rest upon the mesh until dry. Even when dry, larger blooms may need extra support, so use a piece of florist's wire or a floral pick, lay it alongside the stem up to the bloom, and secure them together with floral tape. This will also provide a flexible stem with which to secure the flower to the wreath.

Some vines and twigs may be flexible enough to be simply bent into shape and secured and tied with wire. Thicker, more brittle branches can be soaked in warm water until they are soft enough to be shaped, and then secured in place before they dry.

For a straw or styrofoam form, covering material

can be attached in concentric circles, beginning with the inside circle of the form, then the front face, and last of all, the outside edge. Or you can cover with a series of spirals. Take a spray of whatever material you are using—boxwood, perhaps—place it on the form where you want it, and then pin it in place, starting at the base of the spray, with floral pins. The next spray should be placed so that its top end overlaps the bottom pinned part of the first spray, thereby covering both the stems and the floral pins. Continue this way until the form is completely covered.

Once you have a covered wreath, embellishments can be added in whatever design suits. A rule of thumb is to put small items toward the outside edge of the wreath and larger ones in the middle, but of course, rules are made to be broken. Secure the flowers or other botanicals in place with floral pins, or tape if the stem is weak and has not been reinforced.

Fabric bows, shells, and pine cones can also adorn your wreath or in fact, make up wreaths themselves. Changing the color of the bow will help a wreath segue from season to season, or adapt it to different color schemes. Pine cones in winter and shells in summer also personalize a wreath, and will add interest and texture to plain vine wreaths. Like the colorful wreath of dried peppers often found in farmer's markets, a cone or seashell wreath is a permanent treasure to decorate the walls of your home.

For really unusual, special occasion wreaths, try twining fresh flowers, fruits, and vegetables together. A wreath of sweet peas and roses for a summer brunch, a balsam wreath adorned with strawberries and small white flowers, or a plait of scallions studded with baby carrots and other baby vegetables will excite the eye and add a humorous, creative flair to any decorating scheme. For long-lasting vegetable wreaths, onions, garlic, and dried peppers are appropriate materials for a kitchen or keeping room.

To preserve your wreath for as long as possible, keep it out of direct sunlight, don't let it stay in humid places for long, and dust it occasionally with a paintbrush or a blowdryer on its coolest, least powerful setting. Wreaths can also be stored, again, in a dry place, in a box with silica gels added to absorb moisture.

Ice Candles

The unexpected vision of luminous candles among cold white snowdrifts is the primary pleasure of ice candles. Originally a Finnish tradition, ice candles were brought to this country by Scandinavian immigrants and handed down from generation to generation. As a lovely, natural means of lighting an icy footpath or defining a stark winter garden at night, ice candles deserve to be better known. For guests who have ventured out into the cold and dark, the sudden appearance of flickering candlelight leading them to their destination is indeed a welcoming sight. And in areas where the temperatures remain below freezing throughout the winter, ice candles will last until the first thaw.

Ice candles are supremely simple to make, and might be an enjoyable project for children. In the photograph at left, five-quart plastic ice-cream pails have been used: you may use whatever size best suits your needs. You'll need one votive candle for each ice candle.

Fill your container with water about ½ inch from the top. Set it outside (during freezing weather, of course) until the water freezes — it will take about four to five hours in below-freezing temperatures. The sides and top will freeze first. Just before the entire bottom freezes, turn the ice out of the bucket into the snow where you don't mind water splashing. Nestle the ice candles in gentle snow drifts or along a walk or driveway, then place a votive candle in the center well of the ice.

A Country Sourcebook

The following listing is a selection of sources for reproduction furnishings, fabrics, and accessories for decorating a country home, and mail-order sources of equipment and materials for the crafts described earlier in this book. For larger companies with several outlets, a single address is given which will provide a local source, if necessary.

There are no listings for antiques dealers across the country: they are simply too numerous and their stock necessarily changes too regularly to represent them fairly in a book like this.

DECORATIVE ACCESSORIES

ARTISTIC BRASS
1933 S. Broadway
Los Angeles, CA 90023
Bath fittings

BALDWIN HARDWARE CO.
841 E. Wyomissing Blvd.
Box 15048
Reading, PA 19612
Brass hardware

BASKETVILLE
Rte. 1
Putney, VT 05346
Baskets

BEAR CREEK FOLK ART
P.O. Box 535
Phoenix, AZ 97535

COKER CREEK CRAFTS
P.O. Box 95
Coker Creek, TN 37314
Baskets

COUNTRY ACCENTS
P.O. Box 437
Montoursville, PA 17754
Punched tin panels

COUNTRY FOLKS LTD.
305 Valley Ridge Dr.
Timber Valley Estates
Blue Grass, IA 52726
Decorative accessories

THE COUNTRY LOFT
South Shore Park
Hingham, MA 02043

COUNTRY STORE
28 James St.
Geneva, IL 60134

FRIENDS
Box 464
Frederick, MD 21701

GOOSEBERRY PATCH CO.
P.O. Box 634
Delaware, OH 43015

HARMON BASKET AND
WOODWORKS
P.O. Box 1418
Columbia, SC 29202
Baskets, slatted crates

HARMONY CANDLES AND
GIFTS
G-6429 Flushing Rd.
Flushing, MI 48433

HISTORIC HARDWARE
LTD.
Box 1327
No. Hampton, NH 03862
Brass hardware

HISTORIC HOUSEFITTERS
CO.
Farm to Malker Rd.
Brewster, NY 10509
Wrought iron hardware

HOLY COW, INC.
22 Main St.
Bristol, MA 05443

IRON ART
1122 Hamilton St.
P.O. Box 1794
Allentown, PA 18105
Cast iron toys, animals, trivets

NEAT AND TIDY
27 Pine Brook Rd.
Village of Chestnut Ridge
Spring Valley, NY 10977

THE PAST BASKET
222 S. Third St.
Geneva, IL 60134

PERSNICKETY
Box 458
Great Falls, VA 22066

PIECES OF OLDE
P.O. Box 65130
Baltimore, MD 21209

THE RENOVATOR'S
SUPPLY
Millers Falls, MA 01349
Hardware

STURBRIDGE YANKEE
WORKSHOP
P.O. Box 4
Westbrook, MA 04092

SUNSHINE AND SHADOW
1205 Luanne Ave.
Fullerton, CA 92631

VIRGINIA
METALCRAFTERS
1010 E. Main St.
P.O. Box 1068
Waynesboro, VA 22980
Brass hardware

WHITE'S MILL
MERCANTILE
Box 396
Maryville, TN 37801

FLOOR COVERINGS

THE AGED RAM
P.O. Box 201
Essex, VT 05451
Hooked rugs

THE BARN
P.O. Box 25
Market St.
Lehman, PA 18627
Rag rugs

CAROL BERON RUGS
6 Greene St.
New York, NY 10013
Rag rugs

CAPEL, INC.
Troy, NC 27371
Area rugs, including braided, hooked, needlepoint, rag

CJ ARTS
1374 N. Furman Ave.
Indianapolis, IN 46224

COLONIAL MILLS, INC.
560 Mineral Springs Ave.
Pawtucket, RI 02860
Braided rugs

COUNTRY STENCILER
6 Surrey Trail
Sandy Hook, CT 06482
Canvas floorcloths, wall stenciling

ELIZABETH EAKINS
1053 Lexington Ave.
New York, NY 10021
Custom-crafted rugs

FLOORCLOTHS BY INGRID
8 Randall Rd.
Rochester, MA 02770

GOOD & COMPANY
FLOORCLOTHMAKERS AT
SALZBURG SQUARE
Rte. 101
Amherst, NH 03031

IMPORT SPECIALISTS
82 Wall St.
New York, NY 10005
Sisal, rag and cotton dhurrie rugs, mats

KID-DURRIES/CENTURY
RUG
44 W. 28th St.
New York, NY 10001

LANCASTER COUNTY
FOLK ART
Pat Horfanius
113 Meadowbrook Ln.
Elizabethtown, PA 17022
Hooked rugs

MCADOO RUGS
P.O. Box 847
The Red Mill
N. Bennington, VT 05257
Hooked Rugs

MARIAN B. MILLER KILIMS
148 E. 28th St.
New York, NY 10016
New and antique kilims

MILLS RIVER
713 Old Orchard Rd.
Hendersonville, NC 28739
Braided rugs

JOAN MOSHIMER
P.O. Box 351
Kennebunkport, ME 04046
Custom-made hooked rugs

MULBERRY STREET RUGS
230 State St.
Williamsport, PA 17701
—and—
15135 Sunset Blvd. #220
Pacific Palisades, CA 90272
Braided rugs

DANA NELSON
155 Fairview Rd.
Ellenwood, GA 30049
Rag rugs

PHILADELPHIA
FLOORCLOTHS
510 Merwyn Rd.
Narbert, PA 19072

RAGTIME WEAVERS
4 Jarvis St.
Norwalk, CT 06851
Rag rugs

PATTY READ
3 Alden St.
Camden, ME 04843
Custom-made rag rugs

SHYAM AHUJA
201 E. 56th St.
New York, NY 10022
Dhurrie rugs in patchwork patterns

TRANS-OCEAN RUGS
919 Third Ave.
New York, NY 10022
Area rugs, including hooked rugs

THOS. K. WOODARD
835 Madison Ave.
New York, NY 10021
Custom-crafted rugs and runners

YANKEE PRIDE
29 Parkside Cr.
Braintree, MA 02188
Rag rugs, hooked rugs, quilts

FURNITURE

AMISH COUNTRY
COLLECTION
R.D. 5
Sunset Valley Rd.
New Castle, PA 16105
*Willow and slat furniture, folk
art, rag rugs*

BARN RAISING
P.O. Box 248
Rutledge, GA 30663
Reproduction furniture

PETER BENTSON
Bentson-West
325 Pacific Ave.
San Francisco, CA 94111
*French-style park chairs and
outdoor furniture*

BLUE RIDGE
WOODWORKS
Rt. 3
Sparta, NC 28675
Pie safes

CORINNE BURKE
1 Forest Glen Rd.
New Paltz, NY 12561
Custom-crafted reproductions

CABIN CREEK FURNITURE
Box 499
Lightfoot, VA 23090
—and—
P.O. Box 927
Wake Forest, NC 27587

CALIFORNIA WOOD
PRODUCTS
11281 Goss St.
Sun Valley, CA 91352

COHASSET COLONIALS
Cohasset, MA 02025
Furniture to assemble

COLONIAL WILLIAMSBURG
FOUNDATION
Williamsburg, VA 23187
*Furniture, fabrics, wallcoverings,
lighting, and accessories*

LAURA C. COPENHAVER
c/o Rosemont
Box 149G
Marion, VA 24354
*Reproduction furniture,
coverlets, rugs, quilts, table
linens*

COUNCILL CRAFTSMAN
Box 398
Denton, NC 27239
*18th century reproduction
upholstered furniture*

COUNTRY PRIMITIVES
31 South Main St.
Concord, NH 03301
Reproduction furniture

COUNTRYSTORE
P.O. Box 17696
Whitefish Bay, WI 53217
Willow furniture

FURNITURE GUILD
5095 Riverhill Rd.
Marietta, GA 30067
Reproduction furniture

GEAR INC.
127 Seventh Ave.
New York, NY 10011
Furniture, fabrics, accessories

GREAT MEADOWS
JOINERY
P.O. Box 392
Wayland, MA 01778
*Custom-made Shaker
reproductions*

HISTORIC CHARLESTON
REPRODUCTIONS
105 Broad St.
Charleston, SC 29401
*Furniture, fabrics, china,
accessories*

HITCHCOCK CHAIR
Riverton, CT 06065
Stenciled chairs

PETER KRAMER
P.O. Box 232
Washington, VA 22747
Reproduction furniture

THE LANE CO.
Altavista, VA 24517-0151
*The Museum of American
Folk Art collection*

RAIMONDO LEMUS
125 Christopher St.
New York, NY 10014
*Custom-made Shaker-style
reproductions*

LLOYD/FLANDERS
P.O. Box 500
3010 Tenth St.
Menominee, MI 49858
Wicker-like outdoor furniture

THOS. MOSER
30 Cobbs Bridge Rd.
New Gloucester, ME 04260
Custom-crafted reproductions

NICHOLS & STONE
232 Sherman St.
Gardner, MA 01440
Farm-style furniture

O'ASIAN DESIGNS INC.
1100 W. Walnut
Compton, CA 90220
—and—
3250 O'Asian Way
Charleston, SC 29418
Wicker furniture

OLD HICKORY
403 S. Noble St.
Shelbyville, IN 46176
Hickory furniture

PALACEK
P.O. Box 225
Station A
Richmond, CA 94808
Wicker furniture

REED BROS.
6006 Gravenstein Hwy.
Cotati, CA 94928
Hand-carved furniture

CHARLES P. ROGERS
170 Fifth Ave.
New York, NY 10010
Brass beds, iron beds, enameled beds

THE SERAPH—EAST
P.O. Box 500, Rte. 20
Sturbridge, MA 01566
Custom-crafted reproductions

THE SERAPH—WEST
at The 1817 Shoppe
14659 St. Rte. 37
Sunbury, OH 43074
Custom-crafted reproductions

SHAKER WORKSHOPS
P.O. Box 1028
Concord, MA 01742
Shaker style furniture to assemble

SIMMS & THAYER
P.O. Box 35
1037 Union St.
North Marshfield, MA 02059
Custom-crafted reproductions

RON SMITH
Hissing Goose Gallery
Sun Valley, ID 83353
Custom designing, log furniture, different finishes

SOUTHWOOD
REPRODUCTIONS
Box 2245
Highway 64-70 East
Hickory, NC 28603
18th century reproduction upholstered furniture

TAYLOR WOODCRAFT
P.O. Box 245
South River Rd.
Malta, OH 43758
Farm-style tables and chairs

CHARLES E. THIBEAU
Box 222
Groton, MA 01450
Custom-crafted reproductions

WELLESLEY GUILD
40 Grove St.
Wellesley, MA 02181

WINTERTHUR MUSEUM
REPRODUCTIONS
Winterthur, DE 19735
Furniture, fabrics, wallcoverings, pottery, lighting, accessories

LIGHTING

AUTHENTIC DESIGNS
The Mill Rd.
West Rupert, VT 05776
Chandeliers, sconces

AUTHENTIC
REPRODUCTION
LIGHTING CO.
P.O. Box 218
Avon, CT 06001
Chandeliers, sconces

COLONIAL TIN CRAFT
7805 Railroad Ave.
Cincinnati, OH 45243
Pierced tin lighting fixtures

THE ESSEX FORGE
5 Old Dennison Rd.
Essex, CT 06426
Chandeliers, sconces

GATES MOORE
River Rd., Silvermine
Norwalk, CT 06850
Chandeliers, sconces

HERITAGE LANTERNS
70A Main St.
Yarmouth, ME 04096
Chandeliers, sconces, outdoor lighting

LT. MOSES WILLARD &
CO.
1156 U.S. 50
Cincinnati, OH 45150
Chandeliers, sconces, tin lanterns

PICKWICK PAPERS
4592 Lancaster Rd.
Granville, OH 43023
Lampshades

POTTERY AND TABLETOP

J.K. ADAMS CO.
Dorset, VT 05251
Wooden bowls, boards

BEAUMONT POTTERY
293 Beech Ridge Rd.
York, ME 03909
Stoneware

BENNINGTON POTTERS
324 Country St.
Bennington, VT 05201
Earthenware, including spatterware

BOCH
Comalco International
P.O. Box 675
Perrysburg, OH 43551
Dinnerware, including stickware

BOSTON WAREHOUSE
180 Kerry Pl.
Norwood, MA 02062
Cookware, kitchenware, kitchen linens

LESTER BREININGER
South Church St.
Rebesonia, PA 19551
Redware, slipware

BYBEE POTTERY
P.O. Box 192
Waco, KY 40385

CGS
14180 S.W. 139th Ct.
Miami, FL 33186
Granitewear

COLONIAL FORM
11167 Hillis Rd.
Riverdale, MI 48877
Redware

GRIS POTTERY
10 W. Main St.
Carpentersville, IL 60110
Redware, pottery lamps

HALL CHINA
34 Wildwood Rd.
New Rochelle, NY 10804
1930s and 40s reissues

HARTSTONE
P.O. Box 2626
Zanesville, OH 43701
*Earthenware, kitchenwares,
cookie molds, canisters*

JOHNSON BROS.
41 Madison Ave.
New York, NY 10010
*Earthenware, incl. Laura
Ashley designs*

LOUISVILLE STONEWARE
731 Brent St.
Louisville, KY 40204
Earthenware, stoneware

MAKE MINE COUNTRY
1109 E. Willoughby Rd.
Lansing, MI 48910
Spongewear

NELSON MCCOY POTTERY
Lancaster, OH 43130
Fiesta-type earthenware

PFALTZGRAFF CO.
P.O. Box 1069
York, PA 17405
Earthenware

ROWE POTTERY
217 Main St., Box L
Cambridge, WI 53523
Stoneware

T. BAGGE-MERCHANT
The Olde Salem
Museum Store
626 S. Main St.
Winston-Salem, NC 27101
*Moravian-style slipware and
sgraffito*

VAN BRIGGLE POTTERY
600 S. 21st St.
Colorado Springs, CO
80904
Art pottery and earthenware

VOLLMER PRODUCTS, INC
4522 Macco Dr.
San Antonio, TX 78218
Graniteware

WESSON TRADING CO.
P.O. Box 669984
Marietta, GA 30066
Pottery, decorative accessories

WESTMORE POTTERY
Rte. 2, Box 494
Seagrove, NC 27341
Redware

WILTON ARMETALE
The Wilton Co.
Columbia, PA 17512
*Pewter-like metal dinnerware
and accessories*

TEXTILES

ANICHINI LINEA CASA
150 Fifth Ave.
New York, NY 10011
Embellished bed linens

LAURA ASHLEY
P.O. Box 891
Mahwah, NJ 07430-9990
*English country fabrics,
wallcoverings, furniture*

B & B INTERNATIONAL
13 Old Orchard Rd.
Rye Brook, NY 10573
Throws

BATES FABRICS INC.
Lewiston, ME 04240
Bedspreads

CALICO CORNERS
Funwood Inc.
Bancroft Mills, Drawer 670
Wilmington, DE 19899
Printed fabrics

CHICAGO WEAVING CORP.
5900 Northwest Hwy.
Chicago, IL 60631
Homespun table linens

CARTER CANOPIES
P.O. Box 3372
Eden, NC 27288
*Handmade quilts, hand-tied
canopies, candlewick bedspreads*

CHURCHILL WEAVERS
P.O. Box 30
Berea, KY 40403
Blankets, throws

THE CLAESSON CO.
Rte. 1
Neddick, ME 03902
*Lace valances and panels,
window fittings*

COLONIAL MAID
One Depot Plaza
Mamaroneck, NY 10543
Curtains

COLONIAL OF CAPE COD
Box 670
Hyannis, MA 02601
Table linens, candles

THE COMPANY STORE
500 Company Store Rd.
P.O. Box 2167
Lacrosse, WI 54602
Down comforters, bedding

COUNTRY CURTAINS
at the Red Lion Inn
Stockbridge, MA 01262

1817 SHOPPE
5606 E. State Rd., Rte. 37
Delaware, OH 43015
Homespuns, furnishings,
accessories

FARIBO BLANKETS
1500 N.W. Second Ave.
Faribault, MN 55021
Blankets

GARNETT HILL
Franconia, NH 03580
Flannel sheets, down comforters

GREAT COVERUPS
P.O. Box 1368
West Hartford, CT 06107
Curtains

HALLIE GREER FABRICS
Cushing Corners Rd.
P.O. Box 165
Freedom, NH 03836
Homespun fabrics

GOODWIN GUILD
WEAVERS
Blowing Rock Crafts
P.O. Box 314, Corning Rd.
Blowing Rock, NC 28605
Blankets, throws

HANDS ALL AROUND
971 Lexington Ave.
New York, NY 10021
New quilts

HARRISVILLE DESIGNS
Harrisville, NH 03450
Blankets

HINSON & CO.
27-35 Jackson Ave.
Long Island City, NY 11101
Fabrics, wallcoverings

LE JACQUARD FRANCAIS
200 Lovers Ln.
Culpeper, VA 22701
French brocade linens, towels

JOANNA WESTERN
MILLS CO.
2141 S. Jefferson St.
Chicago, IL 60616
Wooden venetian blinds,
shutters

HOWARD KAPLAN'S
FRENCH COUNTRY STORE
35 E. 10th St.
New York, NY 10003
French country fabrics,
accessories, pottery

KENNEBUNK WEAVERS
Suncook, NH 03275
Blankets, throws

LANZ
Charles Bay Linens
8680 Hayden Pl.
P.O. Box 5266
Culver City, CA 90231
Flannel sheets

LION KNITTING MILLS
3256 W. 25th St.
Cleveland, OH 44109
Knitted throws

MARIMEKKO
175 Clearbrook Dr.
Elmsford, NY 10523
Fabrics, wallcoverings

MILOS MARKETING
111 W. 40th St.
New York, NY 10018
Flannel sheets

MOTIF DESIGNS
20 Jones St.
New Rochelle, NY 10801
Fabrics, wallcoverings

MYSTIC VALLEY TRADERS
400 Massachusetts Ave.
Arlington, MA 02174
Bedcoverings, throws

QUILTS UNLIMITED
203 East Washington St.
P.O. Box 1210
Lewisburg, WV 24901
Quilts, quilting supplies

NANIK
P.O. Box 1766
Wausau, WI 54401
Wooden venetian blinds,
shutters

NEW HAMPSHIRE BLANKET
Main St.
Harrisville, NH 03450

NORTH COUNTRY TEXTILES
AND PENOBSCOT WEAVERS
South Penobscot, ME 04476

NOW DESIGNS
540 Hampshire St.
San Francisco, CA 94110
Table linens, kitchen linens

paper white ltd.
Box 956
Fairfax, CA 94930
White cutwork and lace-
trimmed bed linens

PIERRE DEUX
870 Madison Ave.
New York, NY 10021
French provincial fabrics,
faience dinnerware

POLY-COMMODITY CORP.
175 Great Neck Rd.
Great Neck, NY 11021
Flannel sheets

RAINTREE DESIGNS
979 Third Ave.
New York, NY 10022
English and French country fabrics, wallcoverings

RITZ
40 Portland Rd.
W. Conshonocken, PA
19428
Homespun-style kitchen linens

RUE DE FRANCE
78 Thames St.
Newport, RI 02840
Lace panels, curtains

SCANDIA DOWN
1040 Independence Dr.
Seattle, WA 98188
Down comforters, pillows, duvet covers

PARK B. SMITH
295 Fifth Ave.
New York, NY 10010
Homespun linens and pillows

STEVENS LINEN
ASSOCIATES
P.O. Box 220
Webster, MA 01570
Throws

THE THREE WEAVERS
1206 Brooks St.
Houston, TX 77009
Throws

WOODBURNING STOVES

CONSOLIDATED
DUTCHWEST
P.O. Box 1019
Plymouth, MA 02360

ELMIRA STOVEWORKS
22 Church St.
Elmira, Ontario
Canada N2B 1M3
Also electrical conversions

JØTUL USA
353 Forest Ave.
P.O. Box 1157
Portland, ME 04104

TULIKIVI
P.O. Box 300
Schuyler, VA 22969
Soapstone stoves

VERMONT CASTINGS
Prince St.
Randolph, VT 05060

CRAFTS SUPPLIES

BASKETS

THE BACK DOOR
10 Batchellor Dr.
North Brookfield, MA 01535
Basketweaving kits, reeds

CANE & BASKET
SUPPLY CO.
1283 South Cochran Ave.
Los Angeles, CA 90019
How-to books, caning and basketmaking supplies, stool and chair kits

CAROL'S CANERY
232 Barnsdale Rd. W
Charlottesville, VA 22901
Basket kits

CONNECTICUT CANE
& REED CO.
P.O. Box 1276
Manchester, CT 06040

CANDLEWICKING

GINNY'S STITCHIN'S
106 Braddock Rd.
Williamsburg, VA 23185

THE STITCHERY
204 Worcester St.
Wellesley, MA 02181

CROSS-STITCH

BOYCAN'S
P.O. Box 897
Sharon, PA 16146
Craft and art supplies, quilt supplies

GINNY'S STITCHIN'S
106 Braddock Rd.
Williamsburg, VA 23185

THE SCARLET LETTER
P.O. Box 397
Sullivan, WI 53178
Sampler kits

DRIED FLOWERS AND WREATHS

BETSY WILLIAMS
68 Park St.
Andover, MA 01810
Wreaths and everlastings

CHERCHEZ
862 Lexington Ave.
New York, NY 10021
Potpourris, sachets; also antique linens and other home furnishings

DELICATE DESIGNS
205 Willowgrove South
Tonawanda, NY 14150
Herbal wreaths

FAITH MOUNTAIN HERBS
Main St., Box 199
Sperryville, VA 22740
Herbal wreaths, bouquets

THE NEWPORT HOUSE
P.O. Box 15415
Richmond, VA 23227
Floral supplies, wreath forms, dried botanicals

HOOKED RUGS

THE HOOKING ROOM
1840 House
237 Pine Point Rd.
Scarborough, ME 04074
Over 200 designs, kits, supplies

JANE OLSON
4645 W. Rosecrans Ave.
Hawthorne, CA 90250
Supplies

THE STITCHERY
204 Worcester St.
Wellesley, MA 02181
Also candlewicking, cross-stitch, and knitting kits and supplies

QUILTS

DORR MILL STORE
Guild, NH 03754
Rug wool fabric (see schoolhouse quilt project)

STENCILING

ADELE BISHOP, INC.
P.O. Box 3349
Kinston, NC 28502-3349
Japan paints, brushes, stencil sheets, and other related materials

STENCIL HOUSE OF
NEW HAMPSHIRE
P.O. Box 109
Hooksett, NH 03106
Stencils

TEXAS ART SUPPLY
2001 Montrose
Houston, TX 77006
Paints

S. WOLF'S SONS
771 Ninth Ave.
New York, NY 10019
Paints

FAVOR-RUHL
23 S. Wabash
Chicago, IL 60603
Paints

FLAX'S
1699 Market St.
San Francisco, CA 94103
Paints

GAIL GRISI STENCILING
P.O. Box 1263-H
Haddonfield, NJ 08033
Pre-cut, ready-to-use stencils, stenciling supplies

OLD FASHIONED MILK
PAINT CO.
Box 222
Groton, MA 01450
Milk paints

Index

A

Advertising Art   40-41
Animals, folk art   43, 66-69
Amish Quilts   140-41
Arbor   177

B

Baskets   56, 69, 72-73, 78-79,
   123, 179
Basket Quilt   194-97
Bed Hangings   128, 133, 134-35
Bedrooms   126-57
Beds, Four-Poster   132-33, 144-45,
   150-51
Bleaching   221

C

Candlewicking   210-13
Canopies   128-29, 133, 134-35, 137,
   138
Checkerboards   120-21
Children's Rooms   154-57
Collectibles   56-61, 66-69, 74-75,
   78-81, 84-91, 120-21
Collections, Displaying   43, 56-57,
   64-65, 104-05, 117, 120, 198-99
Color   38-39, 92-93, 110-13, 136-37
Colorwashing   216-17
Combing   214-15, 217, 219
Conservatories   176
Country in the City   52-55
Coverlets   117, 150-53
Cross-stitch   206-09

D

Decoys   58-59, 179
Dedhamware   86-87
Dining Rooms   70-97
Dolls   158-61
   doll clothes   50-51
Doorstops   114-15
Dragging   220

E

Earthenware   84-89, 104-05

F

Fireboards   54
Fireplaces   54-55, 72-73
Flowers, Dried   54, 116, 170, 186-
   87, 234-37
Folk Art   66-69
Four-Poster Beds   132-22, 144-45

G

Gameboards   43, 120-21
Gardens   178-81
Gaudy Dutch   86-87
Gazebo   177
Greenhouses   172, 176-77
Grenfell Rugs   36-37
Guest Rooms   148-49

H

Halls & Stairs   116-19, 122-25
Homespuns   74-75
Hooked Rugs   34-37, 43, 54, 96,
   119, 190, 230-33

I

Ice Candles   242-43

J

Jacquard   150-51
Jaspé   85

K

Keeping Rooms   72-73
Kitchens   98-115
Kitchen Utensils   102-03

L

Lace   64-65, 82, 105, 202-05
Linens   64-65, 148-49, 202-05
Living Rooms   28-69

M

Majolica   54
Marbling   214-15, 216
Milk Paint   55, 132, 214, 219, 221,
   223

O

One-room Living   32-33

P

Paint Techniques   96, 112-13,
   214-21
Penny Rugs   226-29
Pickling   221
Pie Safe   109
Pomanders   236-37
Porches   94-95, 170-73, 180-81
Potpourris   61, 234-37
Pottery   84-91

Q

Quilts   32-33, 43, 52, 55, 116,
   138- 43, 190-201
      Amish Designs   140-41
      Basket   194-97
      Caring for   142-43, 198-201
      Schoolhouse   190-93

R

Raggedy Ann   109, 158-59
Ragging   221
Rugs   34-37, 226-33
   Grenfell   36-37
   Hooked   34-37, 43, 54, 96, 119,
      190, 230-33
   Penny   226-29
   Rag   34, 83

S

Samplers   206-09
Saturday Evening Girls Club   86
Schoolhouse Motif   190-93, 215
Schoolhouse Quilt   192-93, 215
Screened House   174-75
Sgraffito   85
Shaker   40-41, 46-51
Sheeting   33, 130-35
Slipwear   85
Spatterware   53, 90
Spongeware   91
Sponging   218, 221
Stairs   122-25
Stenciling   53, 93, 118, 123, 124,
   125, 222-25
Stickspatter ware   90
Stoneware   56, 87, 88-89, 123

T

Tablesettings   96-97
Teddy Bears   164-67
Toys   68-69, 158-67
Treehouse   184-85
Treen   80-81
Trompe l'Oeil   33, 112-13, 216, 218
Turkeywork   146-47, 156, 174
Tussie mussies   237

U

Utensils   81, 102-03

W

Weathervanes   52, 69
Wicker   62, 83, 106, 170, 172-75,
   179
Willowware   76-77, 105
Windsor Chairs   171
Wing Chairs   44-45, 76
Wood Stove   108
Woodenwares   80-81
Wreaths   238-41

Y

Yellowware   85

PAGE

Copyright
     Paul Kopelow
Contents
     Jon Elliott,
     Jessie Walker,
     Paul Kopelow,
     Jessie Walker
9   Keith Scott Morton
10   Jon Elliott
12   Jessie Walker
13   Elyse Lewin
14   Keith Scott Morton
15   Lynn Karlin
16-17 André Gillardin
18   Jessie Walker
20   Keith Scott Morton
21   Joshua Greene
22-23 Keith Scott Morton
24-25 Keith Scott Morton
26   Keith Scott Morton
28-29 Keith Scott Morton
30   Jessie Walker
31   Keith Scott Morton
32   André Gillardin
33   Keith Scott Morton
34-35 Jessie Walker (left)
     Keith Scott Morton (right)
36-37 Keith Scott Morton
38   Keith Scott Morton
39   Keith Scott Morton
40-41 Jessie Walker
42-43 Keith Scott Morton
44-45 Keith Scott Morton (left)
     Jessie Walker (center)
     Keith Scott Morton (right)
45   Keith Scott Morton
46   Jon Elliott
47   Paul Kopelow
48-51 Jon Elliott

52   Paul Kopelow (top)
     Joe Standart (bottom)
53   Tom Yee
54   Susan Wood (top)
     Jon Elliott (bottom)
55   Keith Scott Morton (top)
     Paul Kopelow (bottom)
56   Jon Elliott (top)
     Paul Kopelow (bottom)
57   André Gillardin
58   Keith Scott Morton
59   Keith Scott Morton (left)
     Jessie Walker (right)
60   Keith Scott Morton
60-61 André Gillardin
     Keith Scott Morton (inset)
62   Ben Rosenthal (top)
     Charles Nesbit (bottom)
63   Paul Kopelow (left)
     Joshua Greene (right)
64-65 Jessie Walker
66   Jessie Walker (top)
     André Gillardin (bottom)
67   Jessie Walker (left)
     Paul Kopelow (right)
68   Paul Kopelow (left)
     Keith Scott Morton (right)

69   Keith Scott Morton (left)
     Jessie Walker (right)
70-71 Keith Scott Morton
72-73 Rick Patrick (left)
     Al Teufen (right)
74   Jessie Walker (left)
     Keith Scott Morton (right)
75   Keith Scott Morton
76   Jon Elliott
77   Keith Scott Morton
78   Jessie Walker
79   Jessie Walker (left)
     Rick Patrick (right)
80   Jessie Walker
81   Keith Scott Morton
82   Jessie Walker
83   Keith Scott Morton (left)
     Lynn Karlin (right)
84-85 Keith Scott Morton
86   Charles Nesbit
87   Keith Scott Morton
88-89 Jessie Walker
89   Keith Scott Morton
90   Paul Kopelow (top)
     Keith Scott Morton (bottom)
91   Keith Scott Morton
92   William P. Steele
93   Paul Kopelow
94   Keith Scott Morton
95   Jessie Walker
96   George Ross (left)
     Jessie Walker (right)
97   Keith Scott Morton
98-99 Jessie Walker
100 Paul Kopelow (top)
     Keith Scott Morton (bottom)
101 Jessie Walker

102-3 Keith Scott Morton
104 Joshua Greene
105 Paul Kopelow (top)
     Jessie Walker (bottom)
106 Jessie Walker
107 Jessie Walker (top)
     Keith Scott Morton (bottom)
108 Doug Kennedy (left)
     Paul Kopelow (right)
109 Keith Scott Morton (left)
     André Gillardin (right)
110 Keith Scott Morton
111 Jessie Walker
112 Rick Patrick
113 George Ross (top)
     Rick Patrick (bottom)
114-15 Keith Scott Morton
116 Joshua Greene (left)
     Keith Scott Morton (top right)
     Al Teufen (bottom right)
117 Al Teufen
118 Jessie Walker
119 Keith Scott Morton
120-21 James Levin
121 Keith Scott Morton (left)
     Paul Kopelow (top right)
     Keith Scott Morton (bottom right)
122 Jessie Walker

123   Keith Scott Morton
         (top)
         Elyse Lewin
         (bottom)
         Keith Scott Morton
         (bottom right)
124-25   Jessie Walker (left)
         Keith Scott Morton
         (center)
         Jessie Walker (top
         right)
         Keith Scott Morton
         (bottom right)
126-27   Keith Scott Morton
128   Keith Scott Morton
129   Keith Scott Morton
130-31   Tom McCavera
132   Jon Elliott (top)
         Keith Scott Morton
         (bottom)
133   Keith Scott Morton
134   Paul Kopelow
         (top)
         Keith Scott Morton
         (bottom)
135   James Levin
136   Jessie Walker
137   Charles Nesbit
         (top)
         George Ross
         (bottom)
138   Keith Scott Morton
         (top)
         Jessie Walker
         (bottom)
139   Bradford
         Ensminger
         Keith Scott Morton
         (inset)
140-41   Jessie Walker
142-43   Jessie Walker
144   Paul Kopelow
145   Jessie Walker (top)
         Keith Scott Morton
         (bottom)

146-47   Keith Scott Morton
148   Ben Rosenthal
         (top)
         Keith Scott Morton
         (bottom)
149   André Gillardin
         (top)
         Tom McCavera
         (bottom)
150-51   Jessie Walker
152-53   Jessie Walker
154   Keith Scott Morton
155   Jessie Walker
156   Keith Scott Morton
         (top)
         Rick Patrick
         (bottom)
157   Keith Scott Morton
158   Jessie Walker
159   Robert Bogertman
160   Keith Scott Morton
161   Keith Scott Morton
162   Jessie Walker
163   Jessie Walker
164   Keith Scott Morton
165   Keith Scott Morton
         (top)
         Jessie Walker
         (bottom left)
         Jon Elliott (bottom
         right)
166   Paul Kopelow
         (left)
         Jessie Walker
         (right)
167   Keith Scott Morton
168-69   Keith Scott Morton
170   Keith Scott Morton
171   Keith Scott Morton
172   Jessie Walker
173   Jessie Walker (left)
         Keith Scott Morton
         (right)

174-75   Keith Scott Morton
176   Paul Kopelow
177   Keith Scott Morton
         (left)
         Jessie Walker
         (right)
178   Jessie Walker
179   Keith Scott Morton
         (top)
         Joshua Greene
         (bottom left)
         Jessie Walker
         (bottom right)
180-81   Jessie Walker (top
         left)
         Keith Scott Morton
         (top right and
         bottom left)
         Rick Patrick (right)
182-85   Keith Scott Morton
186   Keith Scott Morton
188-89   Keith Scott Morton
190   Keith Scott Morton
         (top)
         André Gillardin
         (bottom left)
         Keith Scott Morton
         (bottom right)
191   Keith Scott Morton
         (left)
         Paul Kopelow
         (right)
192   Keith Scott Morton
194   Joe Standart
         (top)
         André Gillardin
         (bottom)
195   Keith Scott Morton
198   James Levin
         (left)
         Keith Scott Morton
         (right)
199   Paul Kopelow
202-3   Keith Scott Morton

206   Keith Scott Morton
207   Keith Scott Morton
210   Keith Scott Morton
211   Keith Scott Morton
214   Joshua Greene
215   Keith Scott Morton
         (top)
         Paul Kopelow
         (bottom)
218   Keith Scott Morton
         (left)
         Joshua Greene
         (right)
219   Paul Kopelow
222-23   Keith Scott Morton
         (left)
         Paul Kopelow
         (center)
         Keith Scott Morton
         (right)
226   Jessie Walker
227   Debra De Boise
230   Keith Scott Morton
         (left)
         Paul Kopelow
         (right)
231   Charles Nesbit
         (top)
         Al Teufen
         (bottom)
234   Keith Scott Morton
235   Keith Scott Morton
         André Gillardin
         (bottom right)
238   Lilo Raymond
         (left)
         Keith Scott Morton
         (right)
239   Keith Scott Morton
         (top)
         Jessie Walker
         (bottom)
242-43   Jessie Walker

Acknowledgments

MANY PEOPLE have contributed in one way or another to this book — the homeowners, the photographers and stylists, the staff at Country Living — too many to thank individually. However, Louise Fiore's tireless work in our archives deserves a special thanks. Smallwood and Stewart would like to add their thanks to Elizabeth Saft.